BIRMINGHAM'S
FIRST CANAL
(1730-1772)

The last lock at Autherley.

The Author dedicates this history of Birmingham's
first canal to his wife Patricia and his adopted
parents Tommy and Henrietta Dawson.

BIRMINGHAM'S FIRST CANAL

(1730-1772)

Dr Ron Dawson

BREWIN BOOKS

BREWIN BOOKS
19 Enfield Ind. Estate,
Redditch,
Worcestershire,
B97 6BY
www.brewinbooks.com

First published by Brewin Books 2022

Front cover image: Brindley Place, the heart of
the canal system. © Philip Pankhurst (cc-by-sa/2.0).

A CIP catalogue record for this book is
available from the British Library.

ISBN: 978-1-85858-746-2

Printed and bound in Great Britain
by Dig Print.

Contents

'Happy is the man who, in the hours of solitude and depression, can read a history of Birmingham.'

The Rt. Rev. J.H.B. Masterman
'The Story of the English Towns, Birmingham'
Quoting Augustine Birrell, Selected Essays 1920, Page 331.

ABOUT THE AUTHOR

Ron Dawson was born Ronald Wheeler in Birmingham's Dudley Road Hospital in 1940. At the age of two, he was adopted by Tommy Dawson, a canal boatman and his wife Henrietta and his surname name was changed to Dawson. The couple raised him and four of their own children on the giant Kingstanding council housing estate. Tommy, his adopted father had been born on the canal and most of his working life was a carrier on the canals. After the Second World War transport by the inland waters diminished almost to the point of extinction and he finished his working life as a canal dredger using one of the last horse drawn narrow boats operating on the midland canals. During this work he was based at Padgett's Canal Dredgers which was situated on the Tame Valley Canal at the point where the canal goes under the College Road within sight of the Boar's Head public house.

Ron Dawson began work his working life as a butcher's boy and for the next nine years he had a succession of short-lived jobs ranging from window cleaner, soft-drinks delivery man, and power-press operator to door-to-door salesman. An interest in history and a serious motorcycle accident led him to study for and gain a sufficient number of GCE 'O' and 'A' levels to gain entry to St. Peter's College, Saltley, in Birmingham to train as a History teacher. It was during this training that he wrote this history of the building of the first Birmingham Canal as a mark of his gratitude and appreciation to his adopted parents for making him part of their family. He went on to gain the degrees of BA., M.Sc., and PhD., mainly by part-time study. He became a Research and Chartered Psychologist, and an Associate Fellow of the British Psychological Society. He was an Inspector-Advisor in two large LEAs, a Registered OFSTED Inspector and Principal Lecturer for post-graduate awards and Head of Special Needs and Habilitation in what is now the University of Winchester.

He has numerous academic and research based publications, many focused upon behavioural and emotional difficulties. His first book 'Special Provision for Disturbed Pupils' was published as part of the Schools Council Research Studies in 1980 by Macmillan Education. His Teacher Information Pack (Tips), also published by Macmillan Education, embraced the whole range of Special Educational Needs was described as an 'Opus Magnum' in a psychological journal review. His interest in child development led him to create the Baby

Progress Guides, a pack of materials designed for parents to assess and promote their babies' development up to the age of two years. He also wrote a regular satirical column, 'The Dawson File', for Special Children magazine.

On his retirement Ron began to write fictional works. He has written two novels and six story books for children. He also wrote and composed a song of remembrance which inspired him to create, write and produce 'The Lest We Forget National Children's Remembrance Concert' at the NEC in Birmingham on the 3rd November, 2018, to commemorate the Centenary of the First Word War Armistice.

The author at work painting his narrowboat the 'Phoenix' in a traditional canal style. The hull was built by Springer engineering and Ron built the cabin. He owned the Phoenix for over 20 years and cruised most of the canal network in that time.

LIST OF ILLUSTRATIONS AND MAPS

Author's Note: Illustrations

Please note that the illustrations used in this story of the first Birmingham Canal were taken directly from very old original documents and texts, some being well over two hundred years old. Even my own photographs which are used are over fifty years old. As may be expected many are not of the high quality and standards attained by modern reproductive equipment. Nevertheless I believe that they were and are worthy of inclusion for both personal and historical interest.

Lock and Split Bridge at Smethwick, 1968. The Spilt Bridge can be seen beyond the lock. The gap or 'split' in the bridge allowed a tow rope to pass through without the need to unhitch from the horse or boat. Note the depth of the lock and the water marks which indicate the lift for boats. Note too the large stone blocks set on each side at the top of the lock.

ABBREVIATIONS

Aris's Birmingham Gazette	Gazette
Birmingham Canal Navigation	B.C.N.
B.C.N. Minute Books	C.M.B.
Birmingham Central Library	B.C.L.

PREFACE

GENESIS AND SOURCES

IN THE preface to his book 'The Canals of the West Midlands', Charles Hadfield wrote *'I shall feel the spare time labour of a dozen years to have been worthwhile if they encourage others to write full length accounts of such important concerns as the Trent and Mersey, the Staffordshire and Worcestershire, or the Birmingham Canal Navigations.'* When I first began work on this story of Birmingham's first canal in 1968 as part my training as a History teacher, my plan was to satisfy Hadfield's hope that someone would write a full length account of the Birmingham Canal Navigations (BCN). On picking up the challenge, however, I was immediately faced with an abundance of material, so much so that it was apparent that a full length detailed account would be far beyond my limited resources as a student at that time.

Rather than settle for writing a very sketchy full length account I decided to limit my study to the history of the first thirty years of the Company. Again almost immediately I realised once again that there were far too many primary and secondary sources available for me to give them the prominence they merited within the constraints imposed upon me at that time. I consequently decided to limit my research and writing to the period from around 1760 until around the end of 1772. This period would cover the conception and opening of the first Birmingham Canal and so might provide a small foundation for a future detailed history of the BCN.

Almost all of the evidence sources used, with the notable exception of the Canal Company's Books, were housed in what was then the Birmingham Reference Library. Much of the information used came from two main sources:

i) Copies of Aris's Birmingham Gazette from 1760 to 1772 preserved in the Library; and ii) the Canal Company's Minute Books, Ledgers and Journals which were preserved by the British Transport Historical Department in London.

CHAPTER 1

THE DAWN OF THE CANAL AGE

IN THE England of 1750 there were three main methods of transport: road, river and sea.

Road: The main motive power for road transport at that time was the horse which was used either for carrying packs up to 280 pounds or for pulling wagons with a load of up to 2 tons.[1] The hooves of the horses and the wheels of the wagons caused great damage to the roads which, in the main, had no firm foundation or durable surface. In general the responsibility for making, repairing and maintaining the roads was in the hands of parish surveyors whose duty it was to ensure that each parishioner in the particular parish spent a certain number of days each year working on the roads. Because of the inadequacy of this system many Turnpike Acts were passed during the first half of the eighteenth century which enabled private individuals to make, repair and maintain major roads in return for toll charges from those who used them.

Despite these measures, England's roads *were reputed to be among the worst in Europe.*[2] and Birmingham's roads were no exception. Generally the roads everywhere were in an appalling condition making travel of any kind difficult and often, in times of heavy rain for example, impossible. Their poor condition also placed severe limitations on the weight of any consignments to be carried on them. Small light goods were occasionally sent by stagecoach, for example in a letter of 15th May 1761 John Boulton informed Timothy Hales of London

---

1   Samuel Smiles, Lives of the Engineers, 1904.
2   Phillis Deane, The first Industrial Revolution, 1979.

that he was sending steel tapestry hooks on the "Stratford Fly" stage. Small light goods apart, the net result of these factors was that inevitably road transport was always slow, irregular, expensive and difficult.

River: Rivers offered an easier and cheaper means of transport than roads, particularly for heavy goods. For boats travelling downstream the motive power came primarily from the river current assisted occasionally by sail when the wind was in a favourable direction. Travelling upstream, however, apart again from the benefit of a favourable wind, was a very different matter. To make headway the boats had to be hauled by gangs of men or, in the few exceptional cases where a towpath was available, by horse.

Again, as for transport by road, there were many obstacles for this means of transport. In times of drought or flood a river could become impassable for boats carrying freight. Also many rivers had been adapted to provide a source of power and/or fish via the construction of weirs that breached the width of the river. To overcome their obstruction to navigation many weirs had a removable barrier through which, when removed, a boat could pass. Removal of a barrier however lowered the level of water behind the weir and so, almost inevitably, weir owners were reluctant to give consent for a barrier to be removed, especially in times of dry weather. Again almost inevitably weir owners would only consent for a barrier to be removed to enable passage on the payment of a fee. If a boat should go aground the barrier could be removed to allow a flood of water (called a 'flash') to go down the river and thus lift and free the boat. Again this could only be done with the weir owner's consent. Unfortunately providing a 'flash' naturally lowered the level of water above the weir and so again it was difficult to persuade the weir owner to open it again to allow passage and again payment was often demanded. The difficulties of the boat owners were further compounded when the barrier removal for passage or a 'flash' dropped the water level above the weir to lower than that necessary for a boat's passage.

Some previously shallow rivers had been made navigable by dredging and the construction of "pound locks" (see later in Chapter 6 "Building the Canal") and to some extent removed much of the irregularity associated with river transport. These navigable rivers were operated on the same principle as turnpike trusts did on the roads in that tolls were levied for navigation.

Sea: The cheapest way of transporting bulky, heavy goods was by sea.

"The sea coast route was the main highway of the British Isles in the 18th Century and that required relatively little in the way of maintenance except to harbour installations......A fleet of vessels averaging a little over 200 tons in weight plied along the eastern coast between the Scottish ports and Newcastle, Hull, Yarmouth and London, bringing coal, stone, slate, clay and grain, commodities whose transport through the miry roads of eighteenth-century England would have cost a fortune." [3]

There were, however, some disadvantages to this means of transport. As now, storms could keep ships in the harbours, and in times of war both ships and men could be pressed into the service of their country.

The Rise of Industry

In the middle of the eighteenth century the beginnings of the industrial development, population growth and structural changes that were to mark the industrial revolution were becoming apparent. Whilst the domestic system of production and the ideas of local self-sufficiency prevailed, the three prevailing modes of transport by road, river or sea were, despite their defects, relatively adequate. With the rapid development of factory and specialised production methods serving widening markets these three modes were found wanting. The continuous growth of the population from the 1740s led to a rapid expansion of many towns, and as these towns expanded so did their demand for fuel, namely coal, (wood supplies in such areas were quickly exhausted) for both domestic and productive use. Unless a town were on the coast the consequence was that the transport costs of coal could amount to more than the cost of the coal itself. The lack of a cheap and reliable inland transport system and the rapid and extensive growth of industrial towns and cities created a fuel famine in many areas of the country.

"The fuel famine of the 18th Century would have stopped the growth not solely of industry but of population in many districts had not means been found for overcoming it." [4]

3   Ibid.
4   J. Clapham, Economic History of Modern Britain, 1926.

The means found for overcoming fuel famine lay in the construction of Canal Navigations. Canals were not a new idea or innovation in Britain and neither was their construction. It is possible, for example, that the Romans had used the Carrdyke and Fossdyke for navigation. A navigable canal had been built at Exeter in the 1560s and an eight mile canal with 12 locks connecting Market Deeping and Stamford had been built prior to 1670. Thomas Steers had constructed an 18 mile long canal with 14 locks at Newry in Ireland in 1742 for the express use of carrying coal. In 1757 Henry Berry constructed a canal on the site of the Sankey Brook which was 7 miles long with 8 locks and constructed for the sole purpose of carrying coal to Liverpool. T.C. Barker in L.S. Presnell's "Studies in the Industrial Revolution" (1964) however alleges that, although the Act of Parliament was to make the Sankey Brook navigable, in reality this was impossible and suggests that the Act was applied for in this form because it was easier to obtain an Act to make a river navigable than one to make a canal:

> *"A scheme for a canal from Salford to Leigh and Wigan to provide Manchester and Salford with a better supply of coal had, in fact, been thrown out at the previous session; there were good reasons, therefore, for making the Sankey scheme to appear as just another river improvement."*

It was however the opening of the Duke of Bridgewater's canal at Worsley on the 17th July, 1761, just four years later, that demonstrated and high-lighted that canals offered a way to greatly ease the problems of transporting heavy and bulky goods. The canal was constructed for the express purpose of carrying coal from the Duke's collieries at Worsley to Manchester. The engineer overseeing the design, route and building of the canal was James Brindley, a fearless innovator and visionary. This would be no ordinary canal and in its length he incorporated a tunnel and Britain's first canal aqueduct. These two innovative features caught both the attention and imagination of the public. It was also an immediate commercial and financial success by way of cutting the price of coal in Manchester by one half. News of the canal rang around the country leading to immediate and widespread imitation. It gave birth to and heralded in what came to be known as the Canal Age.

Once constructed, a canal offered a regular, easy and cheap means of transport (one horse could draw upward of 50 tons along a canal) and delays would only occur in times of the canal freezing or when a technical fault occurred. The development of canals, nevertheless, owed much to the earlier improvements in river navigation; much of the engineering skill and practice that had been used to make the rivers navigable was used in the construction of the new canals; the design, building and use of the pound lock was well established and understood; the improvement of river navigations had within it the foundations for a complete system of water communications and the routes of the early canals, and many of the later, were intended to link the nation's navigable rivers; and finally the existing penetration of the island by navigable rivers had led to plans and schemes for canals to link them and so much of the preparation for such schemes was already completed.

Proposals for the construction of a canal, however, invariably met with much opposition. Mill owners feared the loss of their streams which would be needed to supply the canal with water. The Turnpike Trusts believed that canals would reduce their revenues. The road carriers:

> "saw a loss of livelihood, an argument they backed up with the accusation that a transport monopoly was being created, and that the reduced demand for horses would lead to a smaller demand for oats and so hit the farmer." [5]

Farmers were also fearful that the waterway might drain their water meadows, divide their lands and throw their stock open to theft by Boatmen whose reputation, even at this early stage, was unsavoury to say the least. The desires for the advantages that accrued from the building of a canal, however, generally overcame all opposition. It was found that once a canal had been constructed most, if not all, of the arguments against its building were ill-founded. Indeed, because of the leap forward in trade that usually followed the opening of a canal, in most cases the results were the very opposite of what its opponents had predicted.

The cost of building a canal in almost all cases was far beyond the resources of all but a few exceptionally wealthy men; the Duke of Bridgewater's canal for example, cost nearly a quarter of a million pounds (equivalent to around £500 million in 2021). The finance necessary to build a canal was generally raised by the formation of a joint stock company made up of local people holding

---

5   Charles Hadfield, British Canals, 1952.

shares, usually in units of £100. These canal joint stock companies "*produced a new class of investor; the canal shareholder, a non-participant investor*".[6] Joint stock companies, established by Acts of Parliament, were not new but it was the canal companies, by attracting local investors for a locally advantageous venture that familiarised the small saver with the nature of joint stock investments. The rapid and very high profits achieved by some of the canal companies inevitably encouraged such investments.

This changing pattern of investment norms was just one indirect consequence of the opening of the Duke's canal. Its opening was in fact to have consequences which were to affect the whole life, progress and structure of Britain. It was to have similar effects on the town of Birmingham.

---

6   Deane, Op.Cit.

CHAPTER 2

BIRMINGHAM IN THE MID-18TH CENTURY

TO THOSE of us who know the Birmingham of today it is hard to imagine the town as it was in the middle of the eighteenth century. It was then a small but growing town of only 20 to 30 thousand persons, set in predominantly rural surroundings. It is hard now to imagine the slow turning sails of a windmill set in the open fields at Holloway Head[7] and perhaps harder still to picture the scene painted by the poet John Freeth in 1769:

> *"Of Thames, Severn, Trent and the Avon,*
> *Our countrymen frequently rave on;*
> *But none of their neighbours are happier than they*
> *Who peacefully dwell on the banks of the Rea."* [8]

A good picture of the town and its environs can be gained from an engraving of the East Prospect of the town in 1730 on Page 22. While it shows the rural nature of the town and the prominence of the River Rea, it also indicates a town of some significance with some very substantial public buildings. An examination of the contemporary maps by Westley and Bradford on Pages 24 and 25 while both show the town's rural setting and also provide evidence of the town's rapid and extensive growth over a twenty year period. The two plans show that over

7   Illustration in R.K. Dent, Old and New Birmingham!, Houghton & Hammond, 1880.
8   John Freeth, Inland Navigation. An Ode to the Navigation, 1769.

OLD WINDMILL IN HOLLOWAY HEAD.

the nineteen years between them the town had grown from a population of 23,286 with 3,719 houses to a population of 23,688 with 4,170 houses. The apparently small growth in population compared to the relatively large growth in housing seems to suggest inaccuracy on one of their parts, but nevertheless, it is enough here to show, in the words of Bradford on his plan, that *"This place has been for a long series of years increasing in its buildings, and is superior to most towns in ye Kingdom for its elegance and regularity, as well as number and wealth of its inhabitants."* Furthermore Bradford's 1750 plan also shows several plots of land earmarked for building which strongly indicate that the town as still expanding at that time.

Although small by present-day standards the town was large by eighteenth century standards (note Bradford's words about its superiority to most towns in its number of inhabitants) and despite its rural flavour it was regarded, with good reasons, as one of the chief centres of manufacturing and commerce in England.

The town continued to grow and expand. Sketchley and Adam's directory of 1770 gives a population of 30,804 for that year with 6,025 houses, illustrating a even more rapid growth over the 20 years between 1750 and 1770 than in the previous 20, much of this growth occurring north of the Moat and St Philip's Church. Rapid though it was, this growth was overshadowed by the subsequent

20 years' growth which, according to Pye's New Directory, had a population of 52,250 with 9,500 houses in 1788.

The Birmingham Directory of 1770 classified no less than 90 different trades and this figure excluded 300 businesses which were classified under the general heading "miscellaneous". The bulk of the manufacturers were concerned with the manufacture of small metal goods, especially in the non-ferrous metals of brass and copper, such as the making of buckles and buttons (the two largest and most important Birmingham manufactures of this period), wire, hinges, guns and pistols, jewellery, clocks and watches, files, corkscrews, nutcrackers, swords, toys, the latter being divided in the "introduction" into gold and silver *"trinkets, seals, tweezers, toothpick cases, smelling bottles, snuff boxes, tea chests, inkstands etc."* As well as the metal manufacturers there are listed merchants, printers, booksellers, attorneys, thread makers, hatters, shoemakers and saddlers, platers and enamellers. In addition there were 39 *"Professors of the Polite arts and sciences"* made up of 3 physicians, 21 schoolmasters, an oculist, accountants and writing masters, organists, dancing masters, a carver and a gilder and the secretary to the general hospital. The 20 surgeons within the town were deemed not to fit into this category and so were listed under the separate heading of *"Apothecaries and Surgeons"*. An important asset to trade had been gained in 1765 when Sampson Lloyd and John Taylor formally founded the bank which was to become the Lloyds Bank of today, although the two had carried on banking business well before they became bankers in name.[9]

This vast variety of trade did not go unnoticed by the poet Freeth who was always ready to sing the praises of Birmingham:

> *"For mechanic skill and power,*
> *In what kingdom, on what shore,*
> *Lies a place that can supply*
> *The world with such variety?*
>
> *And Birmingham, for every curious art,*
> *Her sons invent, be Europe's greatest mart*
> *In States and Kingdoms ever stand enrolled*
> *The grand Mechanic Warehouse of the World."* [10]

---

9   Sketchley and Adams, Directory of Birmingham, 1770.
10   C. Gill, History of Birmingham, 1952.

The EAST PROSPECT of BIRMINGHAM.

WESTLEY'S EAST PROSPECT OF BIRMINGHAM; PUBLISHED ABOUT 1730.

The following description of the Town is given on the original plate:

BIRMINGHAM, a Market Town in the County of WARWICK, which by the art and industry of its Inhabitants, has for some years past, been render'd famous all over the World, for the rare choice and invention of all sorts of Wares, and Curiositys, in Iron, Steel, Brass, &c. admir'd as well for their cheapness, as their peculiar beauty of Workmanship.

THE NORTH PROSPECT OF ST. PHILIP'S CHURCH, &c., IN BIRMINGHAM.
From the print by W. Westley, 1732.

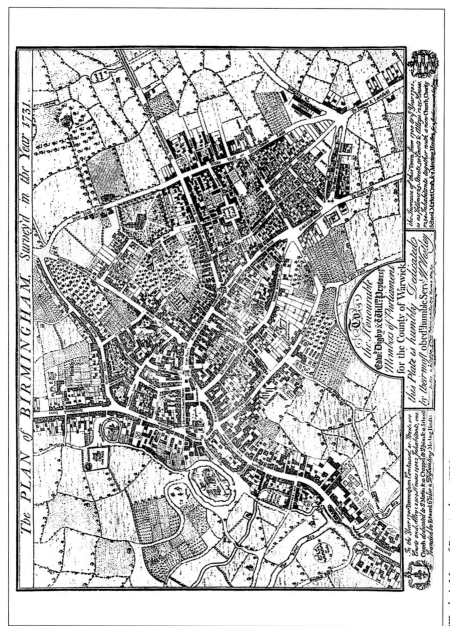

Westley's Map of Birmingham 1731.

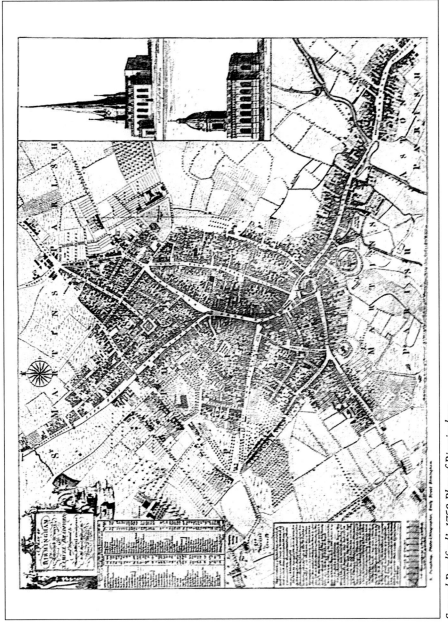

Samuel Bradford's 1750 Plan of Birmingham.

Despite its size and industry, however, the town was still administered as a manor. It had a lord of the manor, at this time a member of the Archer family who still held his rights as a landowner, head of the manorial courts and controller of the markets. The manorial court met at regular intervals to perform the town's business as in a village community. Other than this court and its officials, the town only had the government of the parish which was administered by Churchwardens, overseers of the poor, constables and surveyors of the highways. The system may have had certain advantages in that there were no guilds to cramp or discourage new industries and that in the words of Hutton, *"A town without a charter is a town without a shackle".*[11]

One apparent adverse consequence of the lack of a town charter, however, was that the roads were badly planned and maintained. Hutton tells us that they were of *"such narrowness which scarcely admits light, cleanliness, pleasure, health or use".* The builders were under *"no control"* and *"every leasie"* proceeded *"according to his interest or fancy"* and *"till the year 1769, when the Lamp Act was obtained, there were only two powers able to correct these evils; the Lord of the Manor and the freeholders, neither of which were exerted. The Lord was so far from preserving the rights of the public, that he himself became the chief trespasser. He connived at small encroachments in others to countenance his own. Others trespassed like little rogues, but he like a 'lord'".* He reports that there was on record only one account of the freeholders exerting their rights over encroachment and that was in 1758 when a freeholder demolished a house that encroached on the narrow part of Bull Street.

The provision, maintenance and making of roads within the town was apparently looked upon as a luxury that could be spared and consequently expenditure on the roads was always kept unreasonably low and any capital expenditure within the town was regarded as an opportunity to reduce it even lower.[12] We have seen some of the results in the remarks made by Hutton and if we add that there were no provisions made for the removal of refuse or for drainage we can well imagine their state, and why the carriers issued a notice in 1763 that they intended to raise their price because:

"They cannot carry so much by one third of the weight as they aforetime have done on account of the badness of the roads. It was in fact the bad state

---

11 Freeth, Op.Cit.
12 W. Hutton, The History of Birmingham, 2nd. Ed, 1783.

of the roads that brought Birmingham's first public body into being, for the Lamp Act of 1769 appointed a body of commissioners to light, cleanse, drain, clear any obstruction and to keep a clear passage of the roads within the town." [13]

Life in the town was also becoming more pleasurable as its range of services and amusement grew. The town had its own weekly newspaper, Aris's Birmingham Gazette, which began circulation as the Birmingham Gazette in 1741 becoming Aris's Birmingham Gazette in 1743. A circulating library was formed as early as 1751 and another formed in 1763 which by 1769 was claiming to hold 3,000 volumes.[14] The town could also boast three schools: the Free school of King Edward 6th, the Charity school opened in 1704 and popularly known as the Blue Coat School, and the Dissenting Charity school formed in 1760.[15] A theatre had opened in Moor Street in 1740 to cater for the more cultural visual arts, whilst cock fighting was a regular feature at *"Duddeston Hall, otherwise Vauxhall".*[16]

Hutton tells us that *"the relaxations of the mechanics are news, cards, dominoes, bagatelle and ale in the winter; skittles, quoits, ball, marbles or cricket in the summer, the free and easy, where the buck sports his cash, or consequence, his music or his mimicry, is the resort of many; whilst others attend to pugilism, cock battles, dog fight, duck hunting, bear, badger or bull baiting, according to taste, inclination or education".* He also mentions elsewhere bowling and billiards, the latter, as with cards, apparently always involving a wager for in both cards and billiards *"one man amuses himself in amassing a fortune and another in dissolving one".* Travelling shows with "curiosities" also paid regular visits to the town, for example in 1771 an elephant was on show in the town[17] and a zebra in 1772, the charges for the latter being *"Gentlemen and Ladies 1/-, shopkeepers and master men 6d, poor working people, servants and their children 3d".*[18] By far the most popular pastime, however, seems to be that of frequenting the public house for in the directory of 1770 we find that there were no less than 285 publicans in the town and that this figure was nearly 5 times that for any other trade.

---

13   Gill, Op.cit.

14   Hutton, Op.cit.

15   Gill, Op.cit.

16   Hutton, Op.cit.

17   The Gazette, many times, eg 11th February, 1771.

18   The Gazette, 30th September.

This pleasant picture of Birmingham, however, did not hold true for many of the town's contemporary residents. By far the greatest public expenditure in the town was that for the support of the poor and of the workhouse, which exceeded £3,000 by 1760 (the workhouse was first erected in 1733). We can estimate the great number that this sum maintained when we find that Lady Shelbourne's diary tells us that in 1766 children of 6 to 8 years old were set to work and earned as little as 10d per week.[19] The accounts of the Canal Company for 1768 suggest that the average wage for a working man was about eight to ten shillings per week. Slavery also existed in the town as shown by an advertisement in the Gazette of 11th November 1771 which read *"Two slaves for Sale. One 21 years and one 10 or 11 years, by Auction."*

The Birmingham Workhouse.

Until 1770 the town's links with the outside world were all by road. This was due mainly to the geographical location of the town for although many streams flow out of the Birmingham district, no navigable river passes through it. The two main rivers of the area, the Tame flowing near Birmingham on its way to the Trent, and the Stour flowing down to the Severn, though useful as a means of power, were small and neither was navigable, although Andrew Yarrington claimed in the 1670s to have made the Stour navigable between Kidderminster and Stourbridge. Even if this were true, however, it was not navigable in 1770. The two nearest rivers open for navigation were the Severn

---

19   The Gazette, 18th May 1766.

and the Warwickshire Avon. The Severn was navigable for larger boats as far as Shrewsbury and the Avon as far as Stratford for up to 30 ton barges but both required, by the standards of the day, a long overland journey to be accessed. Nevertheless the Severn, was important to Birmingham as it offered a comparatively cheap link to the port of Bristol. Access to other major ports such as Liverpool, Boston, London, Southampton and Hull, was inevitably lengthy, difficult and consequently expensive.[20]

There had built up by this time, however, extensive land carriage services. The directory of 1767 shows that there were stagecoaches and carriers operating regularly to as many as 168 towns across the country. They operated as far North as York, as far West as Welshpool, as far South as Bristol and as far East as Lincoln, and of course serving all of the major towns within those limits too. Despite these apparently good services being available in Birmingham, the disadvantages of high cost and low speed of road transport were still operative. The cost by stage to London in 1766 was a Guinea (21 Shillings, or £1.05p) and the journey, if there were no mishaps or delays, took one and a half days. Similarly the cost to Bristol was eighteen shillings (90p) and also took a day and a half to complete.[21] Goods naturally went much more slowly and the following account of a journey in the Gazette must have contributed something of a record to raise the comment:

> "By a letter from Bristol we have an account that the goods were taken from Birmingham by William Weston's Waggon on the 8th May at Six O'clock in the Afternoon, were delivered in Bristol by Edward Jackson's Trow on 11th May at 8 O'clock in the Evening."[22]

Thus even when using the Severn, and going down stream, it took the goods 3 days to reach Bristol. Samuel Garbett, a prominent manufacturer of the time, estimated that the cost of land transport from Birmingham to the sea ports added "*from 5% to 10% upon the price for which the goods are sold*", a factor which he pointed out affected the export trade for "*many of these goods are made in other parts of Europe*".

---

20   English Historical Documents, Vol. 10.

21   Court, The Rise of Midland Industries, 1938.

22   The Gazette, 6th January, 1766, and The Gazette, 11th February, 1771.

The condition of the roads did nothing to assist reducing costs or increasing speed. Of the 12 major roads passing through or from Birmingham, Hutton has little to say in their favour. He tells of their constant flooding and narrowness and comments in the case of the road to Dudley that it *"is despicable beyond description. The unwilling traveller is obliged to go two miles about, through a bad road to avoid a worse"*. Although turnpikes existed on many roads, for example that to Saltley, which Hutton especially points out was frequently in flood, few if any improvements were made, and if and when they did in most cases they appear to have only added increased tolls to the difficulty and expense of travel. We can get an idea of the cost of tolls from those of the Birmingham to Wednesbury turnpike which were as:

Carriage by a single horse or other beast of draught	*4d each*
Carriage by a dozen or more horses or other beasts of draught	*3d each*
Waggon with Broad wheels	*2d per horse*
Waggon with Narrow wheels	*3d per horse*[23]

Broad wheel wagons, ie. those with wheels of more than ten inches (25cms) in width, were cheaper than those with narrow wheels because they did lesser damage to the roads.

As now, adverse weather could bring traffic to a standstill. Rains could cause flooding, and snow would often make the roads impassable. The Gazette records that in February 1766 snow *"rendered the roads almost impassable and the Stagecoaches etc were prevented from travelling"*. Travel could also be impeded by the presence of highwaymen; the Gazette records one holding up the London Stagecoach on 27th May, 1772. The high costs of road transport were also attributed directly, though perhaps a trifle unfairly, to the carriers themselves who apparently were held in no higher esteem than the highwaymen, for Freeth refers to them as *"Gripping souls that live by fleecing"* and *"vile oppressors"*.

The high cost of land carriage meant that goods from Birmingham could only be sold profitably at a long distance if they were light and small according to their value, and from what has been said earlier it can be seen that the bulk of goods manufactured in Birmingham were of this type. The raw materials needed for the manufacture of goods were, however, generally very heavy,

---

23   The Gazette, 24th May, 1762.

for example, iron, brass and copper sheets, and consequently the cost of their transport was relatively high. Naturally these costs had to be absorbed in the price of the finished article. All this meant that until Birmingham could gain a much cheaper method of transport, not only was the price of her goods inflated by transport costs but her range of possible manufactured goods was limited and perhaps its geographical marketing extent too.

Coal is a notably bulky and heavy commodity and which was highly desired both by domestic and industrial users within the town at that time. Relatively near to Birmingham there were active and productive coalfields, most notable of which was the South Staffordshire Coalfield which lay only a few miles from the town. This field had nine seams of coal and one of these was no less than 30 feet in thickness (it was often called the Thick Coal or the Ten Yard Seam). This Ten Yard Seam was heavily worked at that time and was heralded as *"the richest and thickest in the whole country"*.[24] The field lay in a wide arc from Dudley, through Tipton, Coseley and Bilston, to Wednesbury and outcropped regularly. This wide outcropping made mining easy and consequently yielded coal that was relatively very cheap at the pit head. The high cost of transporting the coal by road however presented a real problem, for example the carriage of coal by packhorse or wagon for just five miles could double the cost of the coal at the pit head. Consequently transporting coal by road to Birmingham meant that its price in the town was at least double or treble its cost at the pit head. The quality of the coal, however, coupled with its necessity meant that demand was high and the inflated prices were paid. The extent of the use and demand for coal is illustrated by Hutton who tells us that on the road from Wednesbury *"it was common to see a train of carriages for miles, to the great destruction of the road and the annoyance of the travellers"*. A private estimate of the coal trade in 1767 was that some 72,800 tons of coal were brought to Birmingham each year and that some 15,000 horses were employed in the task of transporting it.

The tremendous cost of transporting this very large tonnage of coal can be estimated from a pamphlet of 1765 which gave the cost of land carriage around Birmingham as about nine shillings (45p) per ton for every ten miles.[25] Using these figures we can estimate that it cost upwards of £30,000 per year for the transport costs of coal alone, indeed a private contemporary estimate gave the

---

24   Gazette, 22nd June, 1772.

25   B.A.A.S., Birmingham and Its Regional Setting.

figure as £33,366.13s.4d.[26] Any method which could be employed to reduce these costs would obviously be warmly welcomed and, to those who employed such a method, rewarded with high financial remuneration.

It is perhaps worth mentioning here that beneath the areas productive coal seams were seams of ironstone which were often worked in conjunction with the mining of coal. Ironstone was another desirable but bulky and heavy commodity and so also suffered heavily from road transport costs. There was however little demand for iron in this raw state in the Birmingham of the 1760s.

Early Coaching Bill.
(*Reduced in facsimile from the original, in the possession of John Suffield, Esq.*)

BIRMINGHAM STAGE-COACH,

In Two *Days* and a half; begins *May* the 24th, 1731.

SET S out from the *Swan-Inn* in *Birmingham*, every *Monday* at fix a Clock in the Morning, through *Warwick*, *Banbury* and *Alesbury*, to the *Red Lion Inn* in *Alderfgate ftreet*, *London*, every *Wednefday* Morning: And returns from the faid *Red Lion Inn* every *Thurfday* Morning at five a Clock the fame Way to the *Swan-Inn* in *Birmingham* every *Saturday*, at 21 Shillings each Paffenger, and 18 Shillings from *Warwick*, who has liberty to carry 14 Pounds in Weight, and all above to pay *One Penny a Pound*.
Perform d (if God permit)

By Nicholas Rothwell.

The Weekly Waggon fets out every *Tuefday* from the *Nagg's-Head* in *Birmingham*, to the *Red Lion Inn* aforefaid, every *Saturday*; and returns from the faid Inn every *Monday*, to the *Nagg's-Head* in *Birmingham* every *Thurfday*.

Note. By the faid Nicholas Rothwell at Warwick, all Perfons may be furnifhed with a 'By-Coach, Chariot, Chaife, or Hearfe, with a Mourning Oaach and able Horfes, to any Part of Great Britain, at reafonable Rates: And alfo Saddle Horfes to be had.

---

26 Thomas Bentley, A View of the Advantages of Inland Navigation with a plan of a Navigable Canal intended for a Communication between the Ports of Liverpool and Hull, 1766.

CHAPTER 3

BIRTH OF AN IDEA

AS THE news of the Duke of Bridgewater's canal reached Birmingham[27] it seems likely that few men could envisage such a canal coming to the town. There can be no doubt that most of Birmingham's citizens would have been aware of the great obstacles that lay in the path of such a project. The major obstacle is that Birmingham is situated on a plateau, the edges of which could only be negotiated by a canal by the construction of long flights of locks. As was discussed earlier there was also no navigable river that could be reached by a canal from Birmingham without involving either a very long circuitous route with much lockage or a shorter but still long route with even greater lockage.[28]

The Duke's canal, however, had inspired a plan for another and more important canal that was eventually to have advantageous consequences in Birmingham. On 11th March 1765 Josiah Wedgwood met with Brindley in the Leopard Inn in Burslem (now a listed building) and they discussed the possibilities of constructing a canal from Wedgwood's pottery factory at Burslem to the Mersey or Trent. Wedgwood knew that Brindley had been responsible for the building of the Duke of Bridgewater's canal and was almost certainly also aware that Brindley had also surveyed a line for a canal from Stoke on Trent to Wilden Ferry as early as 1758.[29] The discussion developed into an idea to link the rivers Trent and Mersey via a canal and on 17th April,

---

27 The Gazette, 19th January, 1767.

28 When the B'ham to Worcester Canal was constructed it involved making the longest flight of locks in Britain.

29 C. Hadfield, Canals of the West Midlands, 1966.

1765, Wedgwood wrote a letter to Erasmus Darwin to inform him of a meeting which was to be held at Newcastle-under-Lyme to rally support for such a scheme.[30] In that letter Wedgwood suggested that letters supporting the scheme should be sent by Darwin himself, Thomas Bentley of Liverpool and Samuel Garbett of Birmingham to the organisers of the meeting and which should be read out during the meeting in support of the scheme. Garbett himself went much further than just sending a letter, in that he devised a devious plan to gain more support. In another letter to Darwin on the 4th May, Wedgwood outlined Garbett's plan. The letter stated that Garbett had suggested:

> *"… a sort of mock opposition in the Public Papers to our scheme and the more absurd and abusive the better… I admire Mr Garbett's spirit but I durst not hazard his plan of abuse* [Wedgwood then went on to unequivocally dismiss the plan] *Men are too foolish to be jested with in that manner. The most ridiculous and absurd reasoning will seem serious and have weight with those whose interests lie on the wrong side."* [31]

By this time the idea of a Birmingham Canal had gained a group of ardent supporters and its possibility seemingly more feasible given that there was now a plan for a canal to link the rivers Trent and Mersey. The proposed canal was to be 76 miles long, stretching from Wilden Ferry on the Trent to the River Weaver at Frodsham Bridge, which was navigable to the Mersey. The plan also proposed a branch canal some 28 miles long to serve Lichfield, Tamworth and Birmingham, and in addition suggested that links to the Severn and Thames were distinct possibilities.[32] The Newcastle-under-Lyme meeting was held and it was decided that another meeting should be held on the 27th June and stipulated that it should *"be advertised in the Birmingham and other newspapers"*.[33] Birmingham was undoubtedly beginning to figure largely in this scheme.

The Mayor of Liverpool, however, observed rather pointedly that unless the men promoting the scheme *"were supported with proper assistance from such towns as Liverpool, Manchester, Birmingham … their spirits would certainly flag"*. He went on to state that the canal would *"greatly increase the connection between*

---

30   Collection of Wedgwood letters, B.R.L.
31   C. Hadfield, Canals of the West Midlands, 1966.
32   C. Hadfield, Op.cit.
33   Wedgwood letter to Darwin, 16th May, 1756, B.R.L.

this town and Birmingham to the unspeakable advantage of both, enabling the Liverpool merchants to convey to Birmingham, deals, mahogany, tobacco, sugar and groceries of all kinds, rum, wine and many other sorts of merchandise, and to receive in return from Birmingham and the neighbouring country, all their valuable manufactures, especially guns and other heavy articles at a saving of about £3 per ton in carriage".[34] The Gazette had reported the scheme on 29th April and on 6th May giving some details of the proposed canal; the canal was:

> *"to be 12ft wide at the bottom and 3 feet deep. The boats were to be 70 feet long and 6 feet wide, to draw 30 inches of water and carry 20 tons … the vessels to cost £20 building. One gentleman, it is said will engage to complete this cut for £700 a mile."*

Further impetus for building a canal to the town was provided when the 8th July edition of the Gazette gave details of a rival plan by Sir Richard Whitworth to connect the Severn, Mersey and Trent, *"thereby a communication will be made between the three great ports of Bristol, Liverpool and Hull"*. Whitworth's plan was outlined in a pamphlet which he called "the Advantages of Inland Navigation".[35] The pamphlet contained a detailed plan of the proposed canal together with a comprehensive list of the landowners through whose land it would pass. The plan Whitworth put forward included some ideas of great merit. His canal was to be nine yards wide at the top, six yards wide at the bottom with a depth of five feet and a towing path on either side. The best boats, he suggested, should be fifty feet long and eleven feet broad *much after the manner and form of those made at Bridgnorth on the Severn, and must draw no more than 3 feet and a half of water loaded"*. These would protect the banks, carry 30 tons and cost about £50 to make. The advantage of these vessels would be that *"they will carry goods from Bristol to Liverpool, or Hull, without trouble and fresh expense of reshipping, as those boats now used by the Duke of Bridgewater on his canals in Lancashire will not bear the navigating of the tides way beyond the Hempstones and on that account are both troublesome and expensive, being 70 feet long and 6 feet broad and liable to numberless and immense inconveniences"*. His plan for the canal to join the Severn high above Bewdley, however, meant

---

34 Wedgwood letter to Darwin, May, no day, 1765, B.R.L.
35 Whitworth, The Advantages of Inland Navigation, 1766.

that the boats would encounter three main fords across the Severn. As these lay within a mile of each other, Whitworth suggested that boats could transship about 2 tons into smaller boats for that mile of river and then reship. Somewhat optimistically he proposed that this service could be carried out *"without any additional expense to the person sending the goods"*. Alternatively the three fords could be removed altogether for about £40 each thus removing these obstacles to the navigation of the river completely but as *"the Severn is a free navigation"* its business is everybody's and *"What's everybody's business is nobody's, therefore nothing has been done"*. He also advocated the construction of towing paths along the Severn which would have greatly facilitated navigation on the river.

The idea behind the proposed route was to dig and build two major canals which would form the main arteries of a canal system, all other canals going out from them as branches. Such a branch might go from King's Bromley Common to Birmingham via Lichfield, a distance of some 24 miles. He noted, however, that as the manufactured goods of Birmingham are:

> *"what are called light goods and the quality much exceeding the quantity and I imagine will not turn out as advantageous in Revenue from the tonnage as heavier commodities do [also] as their goods are chiefly polished and wrought iron, they may think the damp that rises from fresh water may greatly injure their sale of them by creating rust and soiling the polished steel… And I believe they would soon choose land carriage for such goods on this account than water carriage."*

He anticipated that the income from such a branch would *"be but trifling"*.

The carriage of Birmingham's light manufactured goods and provisions from the town to the ports was all that the canal was thought likely to carry. If this were to be the case then it seemed very unlikely that this trade could ever provide an income sufficient to even maintain the cut without even considering the necessity of covering its cost. His scheme, not passing through the potteries and entering the Severn at far too high a point for reliable year round navigation, failed to get much of the support that it may have merited.

The alternative scheme, however, continued to find support and stimulate interest in Birmingham. During the Whitsun period of 1765 Matthew Boulton visited *"the Duke of Bridgewater's Works near Manchester"*[36] no doubt wishing to see the mechanics and theories of canal transport in action. In October Garbett was active again soliciting the support of the Society of Arts for the scheme[37] and writing to Darwin that *"nothing less than the proposed canal can support the drooping establishments of heavy manufacturers about Birmingham, Wolverhampton and Walsall"*. About this time too Thomas Bentley was busy preparing a pamphlet for the scheme and on 22nd October wrote to Darwin that *"Birmingham might be made a large article"* as proposed in the pamphlet.

In November of that year Bentley's pamphlet *"A view of the Advantages of Inland Navigation with a plan of a Navigable Canal intended for a communication between the Ports of Liverpool and Hull"* was on sale to the public. After opening with a general discourse setting out the advantages of inland navigation, it went on to say that the most beneficial canals would be:

> *"those which would join the Thames and the Severn, the Severn and the Trent, the Trent and the Weaver, and lastly the Firth of Forth with the Clyde; as by their means the principal parts of our island would communicate with each other. The present design comprehends only a part of the great one mentioned above. It is to join the river Trent near Wilden in Derbyshire with the river Weaver in Cheshire, or the Duke of Bridgewater's navigation, or the Tide-way in the river Mersey, as shall be found expedient, by a canal, with branches to Birmingham, Lichfield, Tamworth and Newcastle."*

To gain the support of the Duke of Bridgewater for the scheme, branches were also proposed to link Knutsford, Stockport and Macclesfield. The proposed route of the canal with the proposed branches is shown below. To follow this route a tunnel more than a mile long would need to be constructed at Harecastle.

The advantages of a canal to Birmingham were summed up as follows:

> *"The circumstances of a water conveyance all the way from Birmingham to the Ports of Hull and Liverpool will be a very great reciprocal advantage to all three places. The reduction of the price of carriage which will take place*

---

36   Letter from Farquarson to Stanhope, 19th September, 1765, B.R.L.
37   Garbett letter to S.O.C. October, 1765, B.R.L.

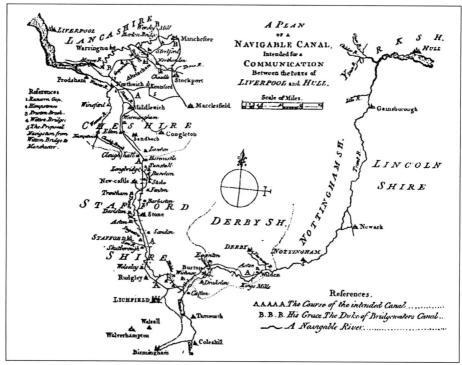

Bentley's plan for a canal to link the Trent and Mersey.

> *between Birmingham and the last mentioned port is so great a proportion of the value of guns, nails and other heavy manufactures of iron, that the exportation of them from that place must thereby be increased to a degree beyond all estimation."*

The pamphlet shows that the plan of a connecting canal to the Severn and so linking the three ports had been dropped by those promoting the canal. This was confirmed at a meeting held at Wolseley Bridge on 30th December 1765 where subscriptions for carrying the plan into execution had opened. The proposed branch to Birmingham had also been dropped by the time of this meeting but several merchants and tradesmen from the town attended with Matthew Boulton acting as collecting agent for subscriptions within the town.[38] In his book, "Canals of the West Midlands" Charles Hadfield writes that the branch to Birmingham was dropped mainly because of apathy in the town. This may have been true but it appears more likely that it was dropped

---

38   The Gazette, 6th January, 1766.

through very practical concerns related to the building and maintaining of such a branch on the part of the undertakers themselves.

The obstacles put forward by Whitworth's plan for a branch from his proposed canal to Birmingham were equally true for the proposed branch from the Trent and Mersey. The fact was that the tonnage of manufactured goods which were likely to pass along such a branch at that time would have been insufficient to cover the costs of making and maintaining it without unrealistic and impracticable tolls being levied. The Trent and Mersey plan without the Birmingham branch went ahead and was embodied in an Act of Parliament on 14th May 1766. With the abandonment of the branch to Birmingham, hopes for a canal coming to the town must have been greatly dimmed but a new scheme was already being promoted which was to revitalise those hopes.

CHAPTER 4

THE IDEA TAKES ROOT
AND BEARS FRUIT

SOON AFTER the Trent and Mersey promoters made it clear that they would not construct a connecting canal to the river Severn, another group of men led by James Perry got together to promote such a canal. On 20th January 1766 the following report appeared in the Gazette:

> *"A scheme is on foot for making a Navigable Canal from Redstones Ferry, on the River Severn, thro- Kidderminster to Autherley, near Wolverhampton, and from thence down the River Penk, in order to join the Canal intended to be made from Wilden Ferry to Liverpool, near Shutborough, which will open a communication between the Ports of Bristol, Liverpool and Hull."*

A meeting was advertised for 29th January 1766, at Wolverhampton. The plan was unanimously approved at the meeting and by 3rd March subscriptions had opened to carry the plan into action.[39] An application to Parliament was subsequently approved at another meeting on the 19th March.[40] The application was successful and an act of Parliament to begin work was gained on the 14th May, the same day as the Trent and Mersey which was to become known later as the Staffordshire and Worcestershire canal. Whitworth's supporters put forward alternative plans to both of the acts but failed to gain approval, and

---

39   C. Hadfield, Canals of the West Midlands, 1966.
40   The Gazette, 3rd February, 3rd March, 24th March, 1766.

the Whitworth plan was eventually shelved although the pamphlet was still advertised for sale in the Gazette as late as 26th August 1766.

The possibility and ensuing advantages for making a branch from this new proposed canal to Birmingham were quickly realised. Such a branch would be reasonably short, would gain access by water to three ports and, more importantly, it would pass through many of the major coalfields on its way. On 14th April the Gazette printed the following letter from a "Well-Wisher to Trade" which laid out the possibility and these advantages for all to see:

> *"Gentlemen,*
> *I Hope this will be no Ways disagreeable to you; please to let the Birmingham People know, that if they have any Inclination to have a Canal from Birmingham to Wolverhampton Canal, the best Way I know is, from Birmingham to Wednesbury, and from thence by Bilston, on the left Hand, and from then to go on the right Hand to Etenshall and by the Coxhead's Farm, and by Blakenhall to Grafely Brook, and from thence to Tetenhall, or rather above the Ways above mentioned on flat Ground; and I think Water plenty all the Way, and you will need but few Locks; you will cross over all the coal works in general; and the whole length of the cut will not exceed twenty miles; and suppose it costs twenty thousand Pounds, please to calculate how much the Coals only will save at Two-pence per Hundred in one Year; I don't know how to judge, but may venture to say one Hundred Pounds per Day; besides, you will have a communication to Bristol, Liverpool, Hull and all other Towns the Navigation goes by, or near; it will go almost close to Wolverhampton; I am certain you can have no Way so good; it no Way concerns me, but shall be glad if such a Work will be any Ways agreeable; you will be freed of most of your heavy Land Carriage; I can't inform you more than know as to Carriage, but I think such a Canal will pay twenty per Cent. Besides lowering all Sorts of Carriage three Parts of four.*
> *Gentlemen, I am your most humble servant.*
> *April 9th, 1766."*

The letter, however, apparently failed to evoke a response, even of opposition, and this may indicate either a general apathy in the town (as suggested by Hadfield) or that the business men of Birmingham preferred to see the Staffordshire and Worcestershire canal under way before they set about to promote a branch to it. News of the progress of the Staffordshire and Worcestershire canal appeared frequently in the pages of the Gazette during 1766. A particularly interesting item appeared on 3rd June when a machine was advertised that 'made' canals, claiming that it could do *"as much work with 8 men as 12 with wheelbarrows"*, and which would *"cut the Time of the Wolverhampton canal from 3 to 2 years"*. The Staffordshire and Worcestershire canal committee advertised the following week for the inventors to contact them but nothing more was heard of it. By 8th September work had started and by December lock building was obviously ready to begin for an advertisement appeared for someone *"willing to make a million of Bricks or upwards"*.

The news and progress of the Staffordshire and Worcestershire canal probably prompted a letter which appeared in the Gazette on 19th January 1767 from a *"Well Wisher to the town"* and the similarity between the pseudonyms of the two letters suggests they may have been written by the same hand or hands. As there are many figures and other information of much interest in this letter it is reproduced here in full:

"The Utility of a Navigable Cut from the Wolverhampton Canal, through the Coal Works, to this Town, is offered to the Consideration of the Public.

By a Well wisher to the Town.

	£	s.	d.
The Average on Coals per Ann, as they have brought			
For some Years past, has been about 5d halfpenny	33,366	13	4
Per Hundred, and the Quantity supposed to come			
Yearly are 72,800 Tons…			
Supposing the above 72,800 can be delivered at			
3d farthing, or 5s and 5d per ton…	19,716	13	4
The Advantage then would be per Ann …	13,650	0	0
But provided 1d per Hundred more is given…	6,066	13	4
The saving then would be per annum …	7,583	6	8

Suppose, to procure the Act of Parliament,	
Purchasing land and providing every	
Necessary cost will be …	*15,000 0 0*
Which sum, to be borrowed at 5 per cent	
Interest, will be per annum	*750 0 0*
There still remain for the Support of the	
Poor, out of the Profits, by the above	
Calculation …	*6,833 6 8*
	7,583 6 8
If the Levies are continued three Years after	
The Completion of the Navigation, at the present	
Rate which is about £5,000 p.a. will discharge	*15,000 0 0*
The principal sum borrowed of …	

The further Advantages that will arise from the under Considerations: It is supposed there are employed 15,000 horses in carrying and drawing Coal, Cokes, Ironstone &c from the Pits; Limestone, Bricks &c from Dudley and its Neighbourhood: Iron, Copper, Block-tin &c from Bewdley and Worcester; Deals, Iron, Flax &c from Burton, which will most Part come by Wolverhampton Navigation when completed.

Say instead of these 15,000 horses, 3,000 Cows were kept, each Cow will produce two hundred and a half of Cheese, the whole Produce of that Article yearly, will be 375 Tons, consequently there will be a proportionable Quantity of Buttons, which are very material articles in this populous Country; besides the great Produce of Calves annually, either for the Butcher or rearing. By a Calculation, from the best information, there will be a saving of 117,000 Strikes of oats and Beans per Annum. To ascertain the further Profits to the Town, that will the Gazettee from the Freight of other Things, exclusive of Coals, must leave to the Calculation of some other abler Hand.

There are many substantial Reasons to be given why the Town should undertake this Navigation.

If this is thought worthy the Notice of the Gentlemen, a Meeting on this Head would not be improper."

The letter brought an immediate response and the following week the constables, churchwardens and overseers arranged a meeting for the 28th January, 1767, to be held at the Swan Inn to consider the scheme and, if it were approved, to appoint a surveyor. At the meeting the scheme met with unanimous approval and it was agreed that "*a proper person be appointed to take a Survey and give an Estimate of the Expense that would attend carrying such a canal into execution*".[41] A subscription was opened to cover the expense of the plan and estimate.[42]

On 2nd February another letter was printed in the Gazette (from a constant reader "A.W.") which gave some different estimates to those given in the previous letter. The writer of the letter estimated that the cost of building the canal, boats, wharfs, etc. would be £20,000 and the profits would be £8,370.13s.4d per annum. From the profits a sum of £5,370.13s.4d could be given for the maintenance of the poor and this would still give a profit of £3,000 per annum. This net profit would pay off the principle sum allocated to make the canal in 7 years' time.

The "proper person" appointed to make the survey was the Duke of Bridgewater's engineer, James Brindley, and at a public meeting again at the Swan (the Swan was the meeting place of the Canal Company throughout the period of this study) on 4th June Brindley gave "*two respective estimates thro' two different courses or channels*" and that "*the upper way or course is the most eligible*".[43] This "upper way" went from near Oldbury, Tipton Green, Bilston and thence to the Canal (Staffordshire and Worcestershire) with "*branches to the different Coal works*", and the estimate for its construction did "*not exceed £50,000*".[44] There are several points in the plan which merit attention. Firstly, that it intended that there would be three terminal points in Birmingham itself; secondly it planned for a tunnel to pass under the hill at Smethwick; and thirdly that two branches were intended to go to the coal pits at Wednesbury and Ocker Hill. At its greatest length the proposed route for the canal was 16 miles, 4 furlongs, 6 chains and Brindley's estimate for its construction was more than double the maximum estimates given in the three private estimates published by the Gazette. The plan's provision for branches to the mines also provides strong evidence that the importance of coal to Birmingham's growth was now firmly recognised and established.

---

41   C.M.B., Preamble.

42   These opening subscriptions were one guinea (C.B.M.) and subscribers were given preference to any future shares.

43   C.M.B., 4th June, 1767.

44   The Gazette, 8th June, 1767.

If there had been apathy in the town previously to a canal, it was now replaced by enthusiasm and action. At a meeting a week after Brindley's report a committee of thirty-nine, including most of the town's prominent men, for example Matthew Boulton, John Baskerville, Dr Small, Samuel Garbett and Samuel Galton were elected, and subscriptions to execute the scheme opened with a condition that *"no person being allowed to subscribe above £1000"*.[45] The meeting also *"ordered that Mr. William Bentley and Mr. George Holloway do wait upon the respective land owners to obtain their consent for making the said canal thro' their respective lands"*.[46] By the 10th July £35,400 had been subscribed and over 30 landowners had agreed for the canal to pass through their lands, many of whom had already signed a declaration of support, and not one of the landowners approached had opposed the scheme.

James Brindley

Brindley's obituary in the Gazette included:

"To these talents (Brindley's) and his truly noble patron, the Duke of Bridgewater, this age and nation are indebted for works which will be a lasting monument to their fame, and shew to future ages how much may be done for the benefit of mankind by one single genius, when supported by those who have it in their power to promote the works these superior minds were born to execute."

5th October 1772.

Promises of support for the scheme had been gained from members of the two houses of Parliament[47] and on the 27th July, John Lane, a member of the

---

45   C.M.B., 27th July, 1767.
46   C.M.B., 12th June, 1767.
47   C.M.B., 10th July, 1767.

Canal Committee, was appointed as its *"agent in London to conduct the intended application to Parliament for the Canal".*[48] By this time the whole £50,000 needed for the canal had been subscribed.[49] More assurances of support for the scheme from members of the two houses had been gained and on 21st August a meeting ordered that *"a Draft of the Bill be prepared by Mr. Lane to be produced to the Committee on Friday 4th September".* Thus in less than eight months after the first meeting to discuss the possibility of a canal, the plan and estimate had been formed, £50,000 subscribed and a Bill prepared with assurances of support from within both houses of Parliament.

To finance the passage of the Bill and the business of the Committee a call of £2.10s.0d (£2.50p) for every £100 subscribed was made through the Gazette on 26th October. As was usual at the time subscriptions were not paid in lump sums but were built up as money was needed by a series of calls which were usually in units of £5.00. The Company spent the rest of the year finalising the details of the application of the Bill. Firstly it was decided on 13th November that an application would be made during the next session of Parliament and that Brindley would be *"requested to attend the house for that purpose".*[50]

To ease the passage of the Bill through Parliament persons who might be affected by any proposed clauses were occasionally brought in to gain their consent. The local coal masters, for example, attended a meeting on 20th November at which they agreed to a clause, *"to prevent the Coal masters getting coal under the canal or within 30 yards of the same, without the consent of the proprietors".*[51] During this period of discussion two important statements were issued: 1, *"that the tonnage by general at three halfpence per mile throughout the navigation"*[52]: compare this figure with the average land transport cost of about nine shillings per ton per ten miles, that is, ten pence half penny to eleven pence (5.1p – 5½p) per mile; and 2, *"that the primary and principal object of this undertaking was and is to obtain a navigation from the Collieries to this Town".*[53]

A letter in the Gazette, however, on 30th November, indicated that not all of the town's population were entirely happy about the way things were

---

48   C.M.B., 27th July, 1767.
49   The Gazette, 3rd August, 1767.
50   C.M.B., 13th November, 1667.
51   C.M.B., 20th November, 1767.
52   C.M.B., 30th October, 1767.
53   C.M.B., 13th November, 1767.

progressing. The letter signed, "T.F." expressed concern about the profits which were to accrue from the canal if completed. "T.F." felt that the committee's estimate of coal tonnage, which he gives as 53,000 tons per year, was too low, but as they are prepared to "solicit" the act for this amount at 3d per ton (this of course was inaccurate for as we have seen the agreed tonnage at this time was to be three halfpence, ie. 1½d) he thought, "*for the good of the Public, a clause should be inserted that if a larger quantity should come, the Tonnage ought to be so much reduced in Proportion, that the subscribers should share no larger Dividend than if that was the exact Quantity, and Commissioners should be appointed, that are not subscribers, to see that every Thing is carried on in a fair and upright manner and proper Accounts kept*". He also mentions the possibility of a clause being inserted in the Act "*that no greater dividend should be made than 10% per annum*". The following week another letter, allegedly from the Parish Officers who had met to discuss the proposed canal Bill, supported "T.F." and advocated a petition be sent to Parliament to oppose the Bill as designed only for "*private emolument*" and not "*the public good*", and to request the insertion of a clause "*to reduce the rates of tonnage in proportion to the quantities of carriage*". The next week, that is, 14th December, however, the Parish Officers assured the public that the letter of 7th December appeared without their knowledge or consent.

The New Year edition of Gazette on the 11th January, 1768, published a letter from "*a considerable Manufacturer of this town and consequently a well-wisher to the Prosperity of its Trade*". The letter decryed the opposition expressed in the previous letters. It asked how many of the opposers "*would have adventured into a branch of Business with a Capital of £55,000 under the same uncertainty of Success*" under the restrictions they wish to impose? Their suggestion of commissioners examining the books is "*alarming to the free-born Englishman*", and he has yet to hear of a "*calculation founded upon the probability, not to say more of the Proprietors ever making more than 6%. Any opposition to the Bill should be avoided for the consequences of the loss of the Bill would be the loss of our Trade, the distress of the Poor*". Inevitably this was answered by another letter the following week the gist of which was that if the canal was not likely to make more than 6%, why should anyone oppose a restriction of 10% and that the opposition did not wish to prevent the Bill but only to gain safeguards for the public within it.

The advocators for a restrictive clause drew up their proposals and delivered them to the canal Committee who discussed them on 13th January, 1768. The proposals included appointment of commissioners to examine the accounts, that interest to the proprietors should not exceed 10% per annum, that surplus profit should be absorbed in reduced tolls or on public use and that every person have power to land coals at a convenient spot at the end of the canal. The Committee pointed out that the present Bill followed very closely the Canal Acts which had already been passed *"and it is well known how scrupulously these Bills were examined in Parliament before they were passed into laws"*. The suggestion of the commissioners was wrought with dangers and they were *"not so sanguine as to expect a profit near so great"* as 10%. They feared too that any unnecessary clauses in the Bill might endanger its passage through Parliament and therefore recommended the Bill remain in its present form.[54] On 15th January a General Assembly approved their recommendation and resolved *"the Bill to be tried for without any restriction"*.[55] Hadfield in his history of the West Midland Canals says the Committee were instructed to accept the restrictive clause but according to the evidence I have seen this was not the case.

The Bill obviously had a quick passage through Parliament, for on 8th February 1768, the Gazette announced *"The Bill has passed both houses for making a Navigable canal from this Town to Wolverhampton and only waits the Royal Assent."* Three weeks later in the issue of 29th February Aris carried the following news item:

> *"Last Friday (ie 26th) on receiving the agreeable News that His Majesty had been at the House of Peers and signed the Bill for making the Navigable Canal from this town to Wolverhampton, the Bells were set to ringing, which were continued the whole Day."*

The Birmingham Canal Company Seal. The seal adopted by the Company at a meeting of 30th September 1768 (BCN).

54   C.M.B., 13th January, 1768.
55   C.M.B., 15th January, 1768.

CHAPTER 5

THE ACT 1768

THE LAYOUT of the Act of Parliament was generally the same as the Canal Acts that had preceded it with only one unusual clause within it. A summary of the Act follows with the clauses in the order as in the Act.

The opening of the Act was perfectly standard procedure and can be seen on the copy of the front page of the Act (see Page 50). A list of all the proprietors followed (see Appendix) who were to:

> "*be united into a Company for the better carrying on, making, completing and maintaining the said navigable cut or canal, and collateral cuts, according to the Rules, Orders and Directions herein after expressed and laid down, and shall for that purpose be one Body Politick and Corporate, by the Name of the company of Proprietors of the Birmingham Canal Navigation and by that name shall have perpetual succession and shall have a common seal, and by that name shall and may sue and be sued.*
>
> *They and their servants are given power to purchase land to make and complete a Cut or Canal navigable and passable for Boats, Barges and other Vessels, from a certain field called Newhall Ring, adjoining to the Town of Birmingham [to go near] Smethwick, Oldbury, Tipton Green and Bilston, to as near Wolverhampton as level will permit to join the one now making from the Severn to the Trent at Autherley, otherwise Aldersley and two collateral cuts, one from the lands of Abney Widow near Oldbury to near or by Girts Green and Brickhouse Lane, and the other from Toll End to Ocker Hill.*"

Power was also given to make reservoirs. *"The said Company of Proprietors, their Successors and Assigns and their agents, Servants and Workmen are hereby authorised and empowered in, upon, or through the Lands and Grounds of, or belonging to, the King's Majesty, his heirs or successors, or of any other Persons or Person, Bodies Politick, Corporate or Collegiate whatsoever (not being, at this time, Ground whereupon a house stands or a Garden, Yard, Park, Paddock, Planted Walk or Avenue to a house, lawn enclosed or adjoining to a Mansion House) to enter and to bore, dig, cut trench, plough, remove, take, carry away and lay Earth, Soil, Clay, Stone, Rubbish, Trees, Roots of Trees, Beds of Gravel or Sand or any other Matters and Things which may be dug or got in the making of the said Cut or Canal."* The Company of Proprietors must pay for any damage caused by their entry to any lands.

The canal, including towpaths, fences, etc, was not to exceed 20 yards width except where it was raised higher or was deeper by 5 feet than the natural surface and in places that were necessary for turning where the maximum was to be 60 yards.

Commissioners were appointed to settle any differences over compensation between the Company and Landowners (among the commissioners several of the company's proprietors were listed, for example Boulton, Garbett and Galton). If there was still disagreement the Sheriff was to appoint a Jury to settle the matter but a novel idea which attempted to prevent a disagreement going this far was included. The Jury were to be paid; if the Jury's assessment was above that offered by the Company, the Company were to pay the Jury's costs, if less the landowner had to pay them.

Landowners could keep any *"Coals, Glasshouse, Pot Clay and Limestone"* dug out in the making of the canal. Mines were not to be worked within 12 yards of the canal and the Company allowed to inspect the mines to ensure this was done, and if violated the coal master was to pay the costs of making the canal safe. If coal could be got, the Company must either give permission or pay for the coal involved.

Destroying the works was made a Felony.

The proprietors were allowed to raise £55,000 between themselves at £100 per share, no proprietor owning less than one or more than ten. If this sum was not sufficient to complete the canal a further £15,000 could be raised by 150 shares.

The subscribers were to receive 5% per year during the workings unless a Majority at a General Assembly decided to postpone such payments.

The Company officers were to be elected, the allocation of votes being one per share, and there must be a committee of not less than 15 chosen at a General Assembly. There were to be two such assemblies per year, one in March and the other in September.

Power was given to make new rules and bye-laws and exact penalties for breaches of them, for the good government of the canal.

The Company was allowed to exact tolls for goods carried on the canal up to 1½d per mile, but Lime and Lime stone was not to pay more than one third of the rates, and all materials used for the making and repairing of roads and all sorts of manure for improving land, shall be exempt as long as they do not pass through a lock when the water is not flowing over the *"gauge paddle or ditch of such lock"*. This clause reflects the recognised importance of farming in the district and also the need for better roads.

A special meeting of the proprietors could be called at any time by 15 or more of the proprietors, giving 10 days' notice.

Accounts were to be kept and *"every proprietor or proprietor, upon every reasonable desire, shall have free access to such Book or Books for his, her or their inspection"*.

Tonnage rates were *"to be equal throughout the whole length of the said canal"* and alterations needed the approval of at least 21 of the commissioners and they were to be given 6 weeks' notice of any intended alteration.

The Boat masters were to give full details of their passage on a penalty of 10 shillings and 3 pence per ton (51p). If there was any difference in the weights given and those measured the Boat could be detained for gauging and if the weight was greater than that given by the boat master, he paid for the weighing, if less the Company paid and also compensation for the delay.

Everyone was allowed to use the canal on payment.

No boat of less than 70 feet long could pass through the locks without the consent of the Company.

If cattle were deprived of watering places, others had to be provided. Towing paths had to be fenced, and gates, bridges and stiles had to be erected to allow passage. Landowners could make extra bridges if they wished at their own expense.

If the Company wished to erect warehouses, wharfs, quays, cranes, weigh beams, etc. the landowner could erect them as long as he did it within 12 months after the Company's request and after that the Company could erect them.

Every boat had to have its name painted on in white capital letters (at a penalty of forty shillings, £2.00 – 2021 value £52.00) and could be measured by the Company at any time up to 4 times per year.

Turning and mooring places were to be provided.

Any wilful obstruction of the canal was liable to penalty.

The unusual clause comes right at the end of the Act. The clause ruled that if the canal did not 'communicate' with the Staffordshire and Worcestershire canal within 6 months of the Birmingham canal being finished between the coal pits and the town, the proprietors of the Staffordshire and Worcestershire canal could complete the communication at the expense of the Birmingham company. This clause may have been added because it was feared that the lucrative trade from the coal pits to Birmingham might remove the incentive to push on to Autherley to complete the intended linking of Birmingham by water to the three ports.

* * *

From an entry in the Company journal for Parliamentary expenditure the cost to the Company in gaining the Act was £770.17s. 6d.

CHAPTER 6

BUILDING THE CANAL

MANY PREPARATIONS had to be made before work could actually begin on cutting the canal so as soon as the Bill had passed through both houses of Parliament, the Company did not wait for the Royal assent before beginning to make preparations for its construction. A more detailed and definite survey was needed and on 12th February Brindley was asked to send two of his assistants to complete this task. He was also asked what implements would be needed and to visit the Committee as soon as possible.[56]

The Committee of course knew some of the implements that would be needed. The actual cutting of the canal would be done by men with pick and shovel and the waste would be carried away by wheelbarrows and so one of the first essential requirements would be wheelbarrows. To this end, the same day as Brindley was contacted, a letter was sent to a Mr Baker of Wolverhampton to ask for a model of his wheelbarrows, and also for his advice on what implements and wood would be needed for the construction of a canal. As nowhere in the accounts for this period are picks and shovels mentioned one can suppose that the men employed had to provide these implements themselves. Much wood was needed for the construction of the canal itself (see later), for locks, and for bridges, and there appeared on 29th February an advertisement for "*large Quantities of Red Deal planks and poplars*" and "*a considerable number of barrows upon a particular construction*". The advertisement indicates that the required advice and model barrow from Mr Baker must have reached the Committee very

---

56   C.M.B., 12th February, 1768.

quickly. Another essential was clay for Bricks and "puddle" (see later) and so on 12th February William Bentley was ordered to look for a bed of suitable clay.

With preparations underway, a regular staff would need to be appointed and so on 2nd March Brindley advised the Committee of the staff that would be required immediately.[57] On 7th March an advertisement for the first staff appeared in Aris:

> "*Wanted, as a Head Clerk or Superintendent to the works of the Navigation, a person who is skilled in such kind of business, and understands Mensuration* [and also an under clerk] *to set out the work, for, and occasionally to work with the cutters, who must be a strong able Man and perfectly versed in mensuration of all kinds.* [Both were to provide] *satisfactory proofs of their good characters.*"

Two applications were received for the Superintendent's post and six for the under clerk and were considered at the first General Assembly on 25th March. Subsequently George Holloway was appointed as Superintendent at a salary of £100 per annum and William Wright as under clerk at £70 per annum. Also at the Assembly John Meredith was appointed as clerk to the Committee at £100 per annum, James Brindley as surveyor at £200 per annum and Brindley and his clerk were paid £120 for their stay in London while gaining the Bill. At the meeting too, the old committee of 39 was replaced by a committee of 15 as allowed in the Act and it was resolved that work should begin immediately.[58]

Brindley's salary of £200 per year is interesting (2021 equivalent circa £36k). Samuel Smiles in his biography of Brindley says that while he worked for the Duke of Bridgewater he was lowly paid, never receiving more than 3 shillings and 6 pence (17½p, 2020 equivalent £32) per day and for the most part only two shillings and sixpence (12½p). Hugh Malet, however, in his book, "The Canal Duke" refutes Smiles' theory and offers evidence that Brindley was paid around £100 per annum and that this was in addition to free board and lodgings and therefore compared very favourably with the salaries of similar men. The salary from the Birmingham Company was substantially higher than both of these, reflecting of course Brindley's greater fame and experience,

57   C.M.B., 2nd March, 1768.
58   C.M.B., 18th March, 1768.

but when one notes that at the same time Brindley was also engaged with and paid by the Trent and Mersey, the Staffordshire and Worcestershire, the Droitwich, and later three other canals, his annual income must have been quite considerable.[59]

All of this work must have kept Brindley extremely busy leaving him little time for formalities. That this annoyed the Committee is obvious from an entry in the minutes on the 14th July, 1769.

> *"The observing that Mr Brindley hath frequently passed by and sometimes come into the town without giving them an opportunity of meeting to confer with him upon the process of the undertaking. Resolved, the Mr Meredith do immediately write to Mr Brindley expressing their dissatisfaction at not being able to see him at such times, and request that at all future times when he shall come to town on the business of the undertaking or to survey the works that he will give the Committee previous notice by a line to some of the clerks, that they may have an opportunity of consulting him upon matters respecting the execution of the work that may appear to them necessary."* [60]

There is no record of Brindley's response.

With surveying and boring for clay taking place, and wheelbarrows beginning to arrive by 26th March, the time arrived to recruit men to do the work and these were advertised for on 4th April; *"Wanted, several Foremen or Undertakers who perfectly understand the nature of the navigation business, and can bring along with them a sufficient number of Workmen, to whom the Proprietors will let the cutting of the Canal in Parcels."* In view of the relative newness of canal building and the large amount of building going on at that time, it seems unlikely that many men who could *"perfectly understand the nature of the navigation business"* were recruited.

No evidence was found to pinpoint the exact date of the commencement of cutting but from entries in the Waste book it appears that such work began before June 1768 and that work on the tunnel at Smethwick had certainly been started by 3rd June, 1768.

---

59   C.M.B., 25th March, 1798.
60   C.M.B., 14th July, 1769.

There is little direct evidence to show how the Birmingham canal itself was constructed but by finding how Brindley constructed his other canals we can get a picture of how the Birmingham canal was most probably built. We may perhaps also find evidence to support the idea that the same techniques were used in Birmingham as they were elsewhere.

As described earlier the actual cutting of the canal was done by men with pick, shovel and wheelbarrow, but at Sale Moor on the Duke's canal, Brindley had devised the following method to ease their labours, speed the work and thus reduce the costs. When about 40 yards of the canal trench had been dug he *"placed deal balks in an upright position, from thirty to thirty-six feet long, backing and supporting them on the outside with other balks laid length ways and in rows and screwed fast together".*[61] When the trench had been made watertight (see later) it could be filled with water and boats could then sail up to the balks while workmen worked on the other side of the balks digging the next forty yards.

The advantage of this method was that the waste dug out, which must have been a tremendous amount, could then be carried away by boat to where it could be deposited. When the next forty yards had been similarly prepared the first balks were removed and that section filled with water. This method was almost certainly used in Birmingham, for on 7th March Brindley ordered *"20 or more planks, 40 feet long, 12 inches broad and 4 inches thick"*, and there was no other purpose on the canal that planks of such length would be needed at that time.[62]

The method had other advantages in that *"the Smiths' forges, the carpenters' and the masons' workshops, were covered barges which floated on the canal and followed the work from place to place"*. Further evidence that this system for carrying away waste and of floating workshops was very probably used on the Birmingham canal exists in the Company Minutes. They show that on 7th April 1769 the Committee ordered 10 boats to be built *"upon proper construction in order that the undertaking may be forwarded with all possible despatch for which purposes the Committee conceive such Boats are very essential".*[63]

When the trench had been dug it could be made watertight in two ways, both of which are described by Smiles in his biography of Brindley. The

---

61   J. Phillips, General History of inland Navigation, 1795.
62   C.M.B., 7th March, 1769.
63   C.M.B., 7th April, 1769.

first was by the use of "clay puddle", and Smiles tells us of how Brindley demonstrated the method and application of clay puddle to a House of Commons Committee:

> *"Brindley caused a mass to clay to be brought into the committee room and, moulding in its raw untempered state into the form of a trough, he poured into it some water which speedily ran through and disappeared. He then worked the clay up with water to imitate the process of puddling and, again forming it into a trough, filled it with water, which was now held in without a particle of leakage."* [64]

In work on the canal, clay was usually reduced to a semi-liquid state called 'puddle' by working and chopping it about manually with spades. It was applied to a thickness of about three feet (one metre) with care being taken to ensure that as each layer was applied it united with the layer beneath it. Puddling was expensive and was generally only used in aqueducts, on ground where leakages were a problem and in places where clay was abundant. The other method of sealing a waterway was by using sand or gravel.

> *"Sand or gravel can be made watertight by shaking it together with flat bars of iron run in some depth, say two feet, and washing down loam or soil as the bars are moved about."* [65]

A big problem in canal construction is of course overcoming the different levels of land. Apart from going right around a change in level by following the contours of the land (not always possible) there are five methods of overcoming this problem: Cuttings, Locks, Aqueducts, Embankments, and Tunnels. According to Smiles, Brindley:

> *"would rather go round an obstacle in the shape of an elevated range of country than go through it. Although the length of the canal to be worked was longer, yet the cost of tunnelling was avoided. Besides the population of the district was fully accommodated."*

---

64   Samuel Smiles, Lives of the Engineers.
65   Samuel Smiles, Lives of the Engineers.

Brindley, as we shall see later, certainly employed this method on the Birmingham canal, although the terrain dictated that he had to use some of the other methods too.

Cuttings and embankments at this time were only used where the change in level was slight and short. Often the soil taken from cuttings would be used to build up embankments elsewhere. In making embankments, the two sides of the canal would be built up, strengthened by driving in oak piles and then filled with water. In order to bring the bottom of the canal up to a level in such a place, Brindley had devised an ingenious method.

> "*Two long boats were fixed together within two feet of each other; between and over them was erected a trough large enough to contain eighteen tons of rubbish. The bottom of this trough was a line of doors, which, upon drawing a pin, burst open and in an instant discharged the burthen. The usefulness of this contrivance was evident; from a near convenient spot the boat was loaded, in a short time drawn to the place wanted, and in a few minutes the whole contents were properly deposited.*" [66]

The time saved by using this method instead of the alternative by men and wheelbarrows can be well imagined. Both cuttings and embankments were used in the construction of the Birmingham canal, although not extensively.

Locks are of course the most well-known and applied method used to overcome significant changes in levels or changes that were long in duration. The 31 locks that were built on the Birmingham canal were narrow locks (ie 7 feet wide as compared to the 14 feet width of Wide locks), but were exactly the same in design apart from that there was only one "upper gate" (see photograph Page 64). A letter of 30th November, 1769, from Dr Small to James Watt tells us some interesting points concerning locks, particularly some of the construction details:

> "*Each lock has cost nearly £300 and they have all been built upon piles and connected to the land on both sides by pieces of wood drove into the land, and built into the brickwork or laced into the land by opening it and then built into the brick work.*"

---

66   Samuel Smiles, Lives of the Engineers.

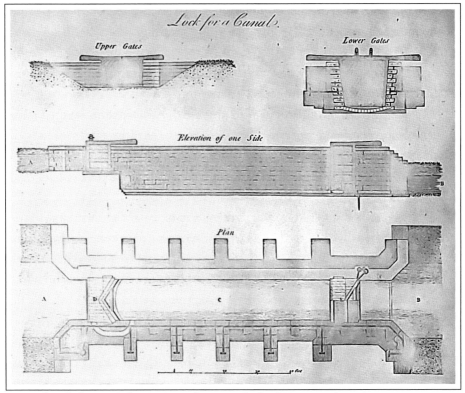

A Canal Lock, from J Phillips 'A General History of Inland Navigation', 1795.

A. *The upper water of the canal.*

B. *Lower Ditto.*

C. *Chamber of the lock.*

D. *The platform on which the upper gates are hung.*

E. *The Lower ditto, showing the manner of construction.*

F. *Sluices through which the water passes into the chamber, to raise it equal with the upper chamber.*

G. *Paddles in the gates, to reduce the water to the lower level. There is a chain bar, run with lead in a course of stone, set at water level.*

Locks were large consumers of bricks and stone and the buying of these items feature regularly in the accounts during the period of construction. They also necessitated the employment of masons, carpenters and smiths and these too featured regularly in the accounts.

Aqueducts were not planned or used on the Birmingham canal but a tunnel was planned originally to pass under the hill at Smethwick. Work on the tunnel must have begun early for on 8th June, in answer to an urgent request of 3rd June, Brindley met the Committee *"at the tunnel to inspect the same"*. On 9th June Brindley reported that, *"having faced and sunk several pits, and discovered running sand and other bed materials for such pumping, Gave it as his opinion that the best way was to avoid tunnelling and to carry the canal over the Hill by Locks and Fire engines".*[67] The Committee agreed and the tunnel was abandoned in favour of six locks taking the canal up to the hill's summit and three bringing it down on the main line and another three on the Wednesbury branch.

The 'fire engines' probably refer to Newcomen Atmospheric Steam engines which would be used to pump water lost from the summit level through the use of the locks back up to the summit level although there is no evidence of any actually being installed. Later Watt's steam engines were used for such purposes, firstly in 1778. As Birmingham lies on a plateau, water was always a problem for the Birmingham canal. Any sources of water that would not bring opposition from mill owners and manufacturers were always being sought, for example, Matthew Boulton experienced a stoppage at his mill in the summer of 1770 because the canal had taken the water from the two streams on which the mill depended.[68] Simcox, Brindley's assistant, gave a report on what water was available to the canal in July 1768.[69]

Following the findings of the report it was decided that the water available was insufficient to meet the needs of the canal and that it would be necessary to create two reservoirs to assist in maintaining the level of the water in the canal. One of these was to be at Smethwick and one at Titford and both were to supply the Smethwick summit. Other measures had to be taken to preserve the water levels in times of drought. One was that in such times boats had to "work turns" at the locks. In working turns a boat going up a lock has to be followed by one coming down in that same lock before another could go up. The result of the method is that a boat is passed through with each filling and emptying of the lock. Another water saving measure was to rule any boat loaded with less than 20 tons could not to pass through a lock without the lock-keeper's consent. Ideas of how to save water lost in lockage were frequently sought. On 26th December, 1769, Boxing Day, Dr Small even wrote to James Watt to ask Watt to turn his mind to the problem even though this might retard his work on steam engines. Dr Small himself had two ideas but he said the one was too laborious and the other too expensive.

---

67   C.M.B., 9th June, 1769.

68   Letter from Boulton to Thomas Gilbert, MP. 2nd February, 1771.

69   C.M.B., 22nd July, 1768.

To cross the canal, bridges had to be erected. There were two main types: those fixed and usually built of brick and those which could be moved either by lifting or swivelling, the latter at this time being one and the same. Occasionally split bridges were also used (see photograph Page 10).

The wages of the ordinary men making and working the canal ranged from six shillings per week (30p) for watchmen to twenty-four shillings per week (£1.20p) for the head carpenter. Cutters got between eight and ten shillings per week (40p to 50p). As in major construction works even today their work was not without its dangers, for example on 24th July, 1769, the Gazette records an incident in which a workman, one John Lester, was killed just beyond Winson Green when the earth suddenly fell in on him. The shortage of workmen because of the surge in canal building led other companies to attempt to entice the men to their works; for example, Bentley reported to the Committee that the Droitwich navigation had been enticing away the stone-cutters.[70] This shortage of men may have been the cause of some men taking liberties with their work, for in January 1769 a number of *"inferior clerks or walking surveyors"* were employed to take daily accounts of the men at work in the different places and to take note whether they were on duty full time or part time.[71] The subcontractors tried at times to get away with shoddy work but the Committee would withhold payment to them until it was put right. For example Fownes and Aston, who did some of the canal cutting, said they had finished their part but as it leaked when filled with water, the committee withheld their payment until they had corrected the fault.[72]

Work on the canal proceeded quickly, as did the work on the other canals to which it would eventually communicate. The following Gazette news item of 17th October 1768 records the progress made:

"The Canal now making in this Town, intended to join the Worcester and Staffordshire Canals near Wolverhampton, is in great forwardness; upwards of five Miles is complete, and it is expected in a Year Goods will be sent from hence by Means of this Canal to Bristol, as that Part of the Navigation from Wolverhampton to the Severn is already complete within four Miles.

---

70   C.M.B., 20th October, 1768.
71   C.M.B., 7th October, 1769.
72   C.M.B., 28th July, 1779.

The Usefulness of this Undertaking, in so populous a Part of the Country, is inconceivable, and it is the Opinion of most People the Proprietors will be great Gainers.

There cannot be a greater Proof of the Advantages which are apparent in Inland Navigations, than the Progress already (in about 18 Months' Time) made in that noble Canal now Cutting, for opening a Communication with the Ports of Hull, Liverpool and Bristol, in such little Time; for we find by the Accounts published, above one fourth Part is already completed, in a Manner far Superior to any Thing of the like Kind perhaps in Europe, which reflects the greatest Honour on the Projectors and Undertakers of that National Affair."

In the December of 1768 it was found that the canal passed through part of the county of Salop and, as this had been omitted in the Bill,[73] an amendment to the Bill had to be sought. The amendment was gained in March[74] and besides adding the county of Salop to the previous Act, it also included permission for the two reservoirs at Smethwick and Oldbury.

During the summer of 1769, with the ten miles to the collieries nearly completed, preparations began for the first boats from the collieries to carry coal to the town along the canal.[75] Bye-laws were ordered to be prepared on 29th September[76] and on 20th October mile posts were ordered to be erected.[77] A temporary wharf was constructed at the Birmingham termination to the canal[78] and on 16th October an advertisement appeared for a man to take charge of it. On 30th October another advertisement was placed for *"a number of carts and horses, for the delivery of Coals in this Town; and horses and men without carts, the company already furnished with some of the latter"*. On 6th November, 1769, the Gazette announced:

"It is with Pleasure we congratulate the Public on the Probability of Coal being brought by Water, near this town, in a few Days; and that the Canal Company have not only resolved to sell the same this winter at their Wharf for Four-pence

73   C.M.B., 30th December, 1768.

74   C.M.B., 10th March, 1769.

75   C.M.B., 10th March, 1769.

76   C.M.B., 29th September, 1769.

77   C.M.B., 20th October, 1769.

78   C.M.B., 1st November, 1769.

Halfpenny per Hundred, long weight, of 120 lbs, but to fix the Price of their Delivery, in every Street thereof: and in order for the better accommodating of the Poor, they have determined to establish coal yards in different Parts of the Town, as soon as possible where, it will be sold in Quantities so small as Half Hundreds or less: And indeed, there is great Reason to believe that the Price of Coal will come (after the present Winter) cheaper than Four pence Halfpenny per Hundred; and that the Gentlemen who have the conducting of this important Affair will use all possible Means to prevent Impositions of every Kind."

Hadfield, using J. Cary's "Inland Navigation" of 1795 as his reference, gives the actual opening date of the canal to the collieries as 6th November, 1769, the same date as the news item in the Gazette. In the company's accounts, however, on 4th November an entry records seventeen shillings and sixpence (70½p) being paid "for drink for 35 men", and this suggests that it was for a special occasion. The proximity of the dates suggests that the occasion was very probably the opening ceremony. A possible reason why the Gazette may have been late with the news is that the 4th fell on a Saturday (a day frequently used for celebration) and as there was no printing done on Sunday, and the Gazette was issued on Monday, the item may have been printed after the Saturday opening through convenience and necessity.

The first boat load of coal was brought to the town on the 7th November, 1769, and the occasion prompted Freeth to publish his ode to the Canal, a sample of which follows:

So quick in performing this mighty affair,
So great was the industry, prudence and care,
Eighteen months have scarce run,
Since the work was begun,
How pleasing the sight.
What a scene of delight
As the barges come floating along.

But for this good care and trouble,
That had nobly been displayed,
For our Coals, this instant, double
What we give we must have paid.

Then revel in gladness, let harmony flow,
From the Districk of Bordsley to Paradise Row;
For true feelings of joy on each breast must be wrought,
When coals under 5d per Hundred are brought.

With coal coming by canal the price of coal immediately fell in the town from between fifteen shillings (75p) and eighteen shillings (80p) per ton to six shillings and eight pence (33p) per ton; and the canal was earning revenue.

The Last Lock at Autherley (1968)

The other side of the bridge is the Staffordshire and Worcestershire Canal. Note single top gate at the top of the lock, the exposed sluice and two ground paddle mechanisms also at the top and a paddle in each of the bottom gates.

In this image the paddle mechanisms in the bottom gates can be seen more clearly. The bridge is typical of the construction of canal bridges. Note the wear on the steps and the iron rubbing strip used to prevent tow ropes from cutting into the brickwork but even this has grooves worn into it by the rubbing of tow ropes over the years.

CHAPTER 7

THE BRICK-KILN/NEWHALL AFFAIR

THE ACT of Parliament had directed that the termination of the canal in Birmingham was to be in "a certain field called Newhall Ring". On 24th May, 1769, however, the Committee ordered that plans be made, under Brindley's inspection, of land, that could be conveniently used for wharfs and warehouses between "*the Dudley Road and the Newhall Ring, and at the land in and near the Brick-kiln Place*", and that estimates be made "*of the expense of making wharves at each place*".[79]

Because of their locations and the undulating lands it is obvious that the canal could not take a single line that would conveniently pass through both the Newhall Ring and the Brick-kiln Piece. Taking the canal to the Brick-kiln Piece would inevitably mean making a separate branch and so inevitably creating two termination points. As this would, again inevitably, result in considerable extra costs this order from the Committee is rather strange. It will be remembered that the Proprietors' original plan was to have three termination points on three branches at Birmingham, and that one of these fell about where the Brick-kiln Piece lay and so this could have been merely a part revival of the original scheme.

The land at Newhall belonged to Charles Colmore. Within the Act there was a clause which enabled landowners to erect necessary wharfs and warehouses and it would seem that he was intending to exercise his right to do this. Clearly the Committee were opposed to this for on 6th October, 1769[80] the Committee

---

79 C.M.B., 24th May, 1769.
80 C.M.B., 6th October 1769.

requested that he sign an agreement to give up "*all claims to erect wharfs and warehouses*" on all of his lands. He refused to sign the agreement but offered to renounce his right to build a warehouse at the Newhall Ring but not on any of his other lands that the Company had not bought off him within twelve months. The Committee's reply was that they were "*not compellable by law to continue the canal to the Newhall Ring*" and that the Company had "*an optionary right to wharfs and warehouses prior to the landowners*".[81] From the wording of the Act it would appear that the Committee were wrong on both counts and their robust reply may have been merely an attempt to bluff Colmore into accepting the proposed agreement. Colmore, however, stood firm.

On 9th January the Committee received a report from Brindley that the Brick-kiln Piece would be the best site for the wharf and the Committee decided to abandon the plan for a termination at Newhall and to replace it by a termination at Brick-kiln.[82] Colmore, feeling that the Act made a termination at Newhall compulsory, "*obtained a Rule for the Company to show cause why a mandamus should not be sought to compel them to complete the canal*" to Newhall.[83] John Meredith, the Company's solicitor, was subsequently ordered to "*select from the Act of Parliament such of the Clauses as appear to justify the company in not immediately continuing the canal to Newhall Ring*" and to pass them on to Colmore.[84]

The Company seemed to be undeterred by the threat of legal action and continued with their plans for the Brick-kiln Piece, and stimulated by a report from Simcox (Brindley's chief assistant) that the Piece was nearer to the principle parts of the town than the Ring[85] ordered "*that a plan be prepared for carrying the canal to and making the wharf at the Brick-kiln Piece*".[86] The Committee immediately began negotiations to buy the Piece. Colmore subsequently applied to a Court of the King's Bench for a mandamus (a writ or command to a lower court) to prevent the Company's plan going ahead but on 28th September the court was unanimous in discharging his application.[87]

---

81   C.M.B., 20th October, 1769.
82   C.M.B., 9th January, 1770.
83   C.M.B., 23rd February, 1770.
84   C.M.B., 23rd March, 1770.
85   C.M.B., 20th April, 1770.
86   C.M.B., 28th September, 1770.
87   C.M.B., 28th September, 1770.

The Company apparently based their defence on the unsuitability of Colmore's land for canal construction and had decided as early as February that a law suit could be decided by engineers' reports. The committee, besides getting reports from Smeaton and Brindley, had ordered Dr Small to write to James Watt for his opinion also. In the letter Small wrote that:

> *"What you will have chiefly to judge of will be the expense and possibility of making a perfectly water tight canal for about a quarter of a mile on the side of a hill consisting of very soft sandstone with innumerable large chinks in all directions. The sand stone may be crumbled between two fingers very easily and becomes more pliable when soaked in water… Clay and Stone are distant dear."*

Colmore was obviously prepared for such a defence, for Samuel Garbett, one of the original promoters and proprietors of the Birmingham Canal who was supporting Colmore in this affair, was in Watt's neighbourhood at that time with the alleged intention (alleged by Small) of gaining Watt's support for Colmore's case.[88] Following the court's decision in their favour, the Company began negotiating again to buy the Brick-kiln Piece and these were finally settled on 7th December 1770.[89]

Colmore, however, had not yet abandoned his case and applied to Parliament for an order to be made to compel the Company to abide by the terms of the act. The fact that the three terminations originally planned by the proprietors were reduced in the Act to one, in the Newhall Ring, probably indicates that Colmore had some influential friends in Parliament. A plan of the proposed and original termination was drawn up which appeared to denote that the Company was taking particular pains to avoid any of Colmore's lands and involving a very sharp bend to do so. Neither was the committee following Brindley's report of 9th January which said the best route to the Piece was through *"Mr. Baker's lands"* which were not even shown on the plan.

The Company sought support from M.P.s presenting their case again on the grounds that the land to Newhall was unsuitable to carry a canal and the effects would be harmful. A good example is seen in a letter of 2nd February

---

88   Letter from Dr Small to James Watt, 26th February, 1770.
89   C.M.B., 7th December, 1770.

1771 from Matthew Boulton to Thomas Gilbert M.P. complaining that his mill was half stopped the previous summer through water being taken for the canal. He had kept patience, he wrote, because he had been flattering himself:

> "... that some means or other would be devised to put a stop to the present leakage of the canal; but au contraire, I am now alarmed with the apprehension of an increase in the extension of the canal into the same sort of ground that is the cause of the present leakage. The very holes which Mr. Smeaton hath dug in Newhall Ring to try the ground, drink up the water nearly as fast as you can pour it in, however, let Mr. Smeaton or Brindley, or all the engineers on earth give evidence they will before Parliament, I am convinced from last summer's experience that if the proprietors of the canal continue to take the two streams upon which my mill depends, it is ruined; I might as well have built it on the summit of the hill. And on the other hand if the proprietors do not take it, their scheme may be ruined. That part of the canal which leaks the most doth extend a quarter of a mile and adjoins Mr. Colmore's land, so that if it should be continued a quarter of a mile further through ground of the same sort, there is no doubt but that the grievance will be doubled; and the present is not bearable; for I have laid out on my stream £20,000 in buildings, machines and tools. I have 700 people employed in my manufactory and more in a consequence of it. People would become employed and foreign orders not met and he himself, deprived of his very existence to gratify the whim of a single man in a matter that cannot produce the least convenience to the publick or even to himself."

He closed by begging Gilbert to save him from destruction.

Despite Boulton's eloquent plea, Colmore gained an Act in March 1771 to compel the Company to make and complete a canal from its present termination in the Free School lands to the Newhall Ring field on or before the 25th March 1772 and that it was to be always kept open and navigable. Colmore had won. The company however did not accept their defeat gracefully and was determined to give Colmore no more than was absolutely necessary. A jury had to decide what was to be built opposite Friday Street. Its decision was that if Colmore wanted anything more than a swivel bridge then he would have to pay any consequent additional expenses including the extra cost of cutting the

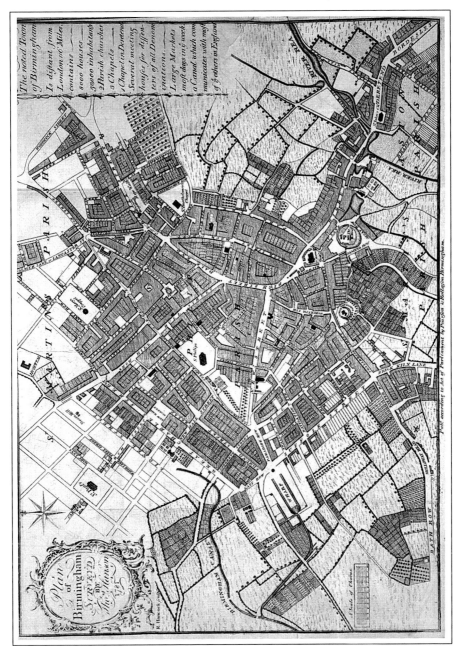

Hanson's 1781 Plan of Birmingham.

banks upright to enable the construction of a wharf.[90] There was nothing to prevent the termination to Brick-kiln being completed and consequently when this was done the Piece became the Company's main terminal point and wharf.

A contemporary plan of the termination of the canal at the Brick-kiln as ordered by the act shows that much tunnelling would be required to reach the Brick-kiln but when the work was actually carried out no tunnelling was needed at all. All in all the plan seems to have purposely set out to support Colmore's case that rent was to be paid to him for land taken in making and finishing the canal.

A later plan of the town by Hanson in 1781 (see Page 69) shows that, although Colmore may have won the battle, he eventually lost the war. At the Brick-kiln the plan shows an extensive and developed wharf with nearby iron foundries near it while at Newhall itself the plan shows little except an abrupt end to the canal and one wharf, Crosby's wharf, lying on Colmore's land.

Overall the evidence seems to show that the Company were quite prepared to take the canal to Newhall, they even took a house to be used as an office there in March 1769 until Colmore refused to give up his rights to construct wharfs and warehouses. Only when Colmore had asked for the support of the law did the Company apparently put forward the case that the land to Newhall was unsuitable; and, unsuitable or not, when they were compelled to finish it to Newhall, the job was done without any apparent harmful effects to the canal or Boulton's mill. Throughout they appeared to adopt an arrogant and uncompromising attitude and the cause of the affair was almost certainly a desire to establish a monopoly of the wharfs in the town. These things did not go entirely unnoticed in the town, and as we shall see in the next chapter, this controversy may have given rise to another.

---

90   C.M.B., 2nd September, 1771.

CHAPTER 8

MONOPOLY AND OPPOSITION

ON THE day that the Committee sent their reply to Colmore that they had an *"optionary right to wharfs and warehouses prior to landowners"*, they also passed two important resolutions that were to provoke great controversy within the town and to a certain extent within the company itself. They were:

1) *"The Committee do upon the whole course of the Canal fix wharfs at all places where they can be of public convenience, and prevent landowners erecting wharfs at such places until the subject is duly considered by a General Assembly, and that proper orders be given to prevent boatmen unloading at any other places than are fixed by the Committee."*

2) *"That for the support of regularity in the delivery of Coals to prevent impositions on the country by persons possessing wharfs without being restrained to certain rules which are on experience may be requisite for the public good, it is necessary that the Committee should exert such powers as the law hath given them to obtain the sole possession of all convenient landing places in order to establish the best and most distinct rules possible for public accommodation."* [91]

These two resolutions, if carried, would give the Company complete control of the carrying trade and a complete monopoly of the wharfs. The Committee also resolved to carry on the whole business of coal trading, buying, carrying,

---

91 C.M.B., 20th October, 1769.

distributing and selling to increase their profits and their advantageous position would make a monopoly in the coal trade very possible. In this respect the Company broke with the general rule that canal companies did not act as carriers. The business of Canal Companies was to build and maintain their canal for use by carriers and the Companies were to derive revenue only from the tolls levied. This attempt to maximise their possible profits from the Canal is a reflection of the hard-headed Birmingham business men who were behind the Canal Company and who were prepared to grasp any chance of financial gain that presented itself.

It seems probable, however, that the resolutions did not gain the unanimous approval of the Committee. A dispute immediately arose between William Bentley, the chairman, and Samuel Garbett (whom Dickenson in his biography of Boulton called "the most public spirited man in Birmingham") and probably stemmed from these resolutions and the Committee's reply to Colmore. Garbett had apparently pressed for the price of coal to be kept low and for the poor to be supplied before all others, while Bentley accused him of trying to gain a satisfactory supply for his own use. The dispute was technically settled at a meeting of 4th December when the Committee passed a resolution exonerating Garbett from blame and showing that the dispute was merely the result of a misunderstanding.[92] Garbett, however, must have felt unhappy about the way the Committee was proceeding and resigned from it before the end of December, John Turner also resigning with him.[93] Garbett soon after sold all his shares, bar one, to Dr Small, and gave active support to Colmore in his case against the Company.[94]

The dispute of Brick-kiln and Newhall illustrated to the town the Company's probable intentions and this, coupled with the alleged and unfair treatment of certain landowners and coal masters, led to a public controversy breaking out in the columns of the Gazette in November. The controversy started with an advertisement of 19th November calling for a meeting of the landowners near the canal between Birmingham and Bilston at the Swan in Dudley:

> "to examine into the manner with which the Birmingham Canal Company
> have conducted some of their operations, and to collect an account of such

---

92   C.M.B., 4th December, 1769.
93   C.M.B., 29th December, 1769.
94   Letter from Small to Watt, 26th February, 1770.

hardships and inconveniences as may appear likely to be redressed by Parliament." [95] The following week *"the Coal masters, Navigators and Dealers in Coal"* were called to a meeting *"to consider upon methods to obtain a free navigation and a proper use of the banks, on the Birmingham Canal together with free access thereto from the neighbouring collieries, independent of the Canal Company; and likewise for the liberty to make Basins or By-stands for Boats to load and unload; And also to make collateral outs from the coal pits to the Banks of the Canal and into the Canal, when the same can be done without injury to the Proprietors thereof, and to obtain proper wharfs at Birmingham where stacks of Coal may be kept in the Winter: And to consider upon an application to Parliament for all possible accommodation to Coal masters, Navigators and Dealers in Coal and that it may be in every respect free of monopolies."* [96]

Much dissatisfaction was expressed at the meeting and another meeting was called for 11th December to discuss the representation that the Company in *"their proceedings have been arbitrary and oppressive, and that having the power, they have also shown the inclination to establish a dangerous monopoly"*.[97]

A letter in Aris on the 3rd December[98] gave some support for the Company, saying that as the canal itself was not yet finished, many of the improvements desired cannot be expected to be finished already, and that so extensive a plan could not be executed without *"some individuals sustaining temporary injury"*. Not only that, up until then no injured party had ever applied for a jury or the Commissioners to right any wrong that had been done. The following week the Committee issued a notice that they would speedily settle and discharge any real grievances that were brought. In the same issue it was also announced that, as the Committee had agreed:

"to establish such rules as may be for the common good of the country and... that collateral cuts shall be allowed to be made into the Canal upon unquestionable security being given that no damage can thereby arise to the navigation or the banks."

---

95   The Gazette, 19th November, 1770.
96   The Gazette, 26th November, 1770.
97   The Gazette, 3rd December, 1770.
98   The Gazette, 3rd December, 1770.

The meeting of the 11th was subsequently deferred.[99] The following week the Committee expressed their disappointment at the meeting being deferred for they had hoped to disprove the charge made against them and declared that they had no part in its being deferred for the assurances they had always given.[100]

The representations that would have been discussed at the deferred meeting were *"offered for the consideration of the public"* by the anonymous writer of a letter published in the Gazette on the 24th December. It declared that at an earlier meeting on 23rd of November twenty persons had levelled complaints against the company, thirteen saying their lands had been entered without their consent and the other seven that their lands had been entered after they had withheld their consent. None had received any compensation. One of the complainants, Messrs. Nicklin and Company, Coal masters, claimed they had been refused access to the canal because they would not contract their coal to the Canal Company. Another Messrs. Gilbert, Fownes and Company claimed likewise and produced the draft of an agreement drawn up by the Company's secretary to substantiate their claim.

The resolutions passed at that meeting were: that the wharfs should be free of monopoly, even of the landowners; that collateral cuts should be allowed as long as no damage is done to the canal; that if the Company continue as traders they should not be entitled to any penalties for violation of their Bye-laws, the money instead should go to some public use; that bye-laws affecting the public should be made by the commissioners or other indifferent persons; and that the canal Company should be prevented from making a monopoly or *"showing partiality to their own connections and interests"*. In addition to these points, the following would also have been raised at the meeting: to avoid an expense of £1,000 to £2,000 had not the Company *"made the canal so crooked as to occasion a great addition to the length thereof; and whether by this means it is not probable they will soon gain more than £500 a year by the additional tax thereby occasioned on Coal only and whether there is not reason to suppose the Public ought not to have some batement on this account; hath not the parish a better claim"* to wharfs, warehouses and weighing machines in Birmingham; and should the Company have the sole rights of granting water for passage, collateral cuts and making bye-laws.[101]

---

99   The Gazette, 10th December, 1770.
100 The Gazette, 17th December, 1770.
101 The Gazette, 3rd December, 1770.

A letter in support of the Company appeared the Gazette issue of the 31st December. The writer admitted that 20 landowners held grievances but "*it is not to be wondered at that out of between 2 and 300 landowners and tenants, whose property lay in the course of the canal, there is not thrice the number of twenty complainants*". Also if there were grievances, what have they to do with the public, "*if the Company have trespassed on the rights of anyone, the law is open to punish them for it*". It also transpired that the Nicklins, one of the two complainants against the Company referred to earlier, had "*refused to pay the extraordinary expense that would attend taking the canal out of its course after they had repeatedly promised to do so*". In the case of the other complainant company highlighted, Messrs. Gilbert Fownes and Company, had suggested the contested contract themselves.

It was however impossible for the Company to establish "*a dangerous monopoly*" even if they wished to, for to do so would necessitate their owning of all the coal mines on each side of the canal. In response to the other proposals, it might be "*asked with equal propriety, whether the parish have not a better claim to the profits arising from the Canal than the Canal Company*". Finally, should the Company be deprived "*of the Powers given them by the legislature before those powers have been abused?*"

In the same issue of the Gazette, however, was another anonymous letter supporting the writer of the letter of the 24th, saying that the writer should have the gratitude of the public and that he has information that doubts have often been silenced in the Canal Committee by the question "*Who will call us to account?*" It also restated the case against the Company for bringing about the loss of revenue from the public weighing machine which was used for the upkeep of the poor.

On 7th January 1771, a letter from Samuel Garbett announced that he had been the anonymous author of the two letters published in the Gazette issues of the 24th and 31st of December which criticised the operations of the Canal Company Committee. His motivation for sending them anonymously and then issuing this revelation is difficult to explain and so remains open to speculation.[102]

In the following week's issue the Committee informed Garbett that, as they had always assured speedy redress to all real grievances they do not

---

102 The Gazette, 14th January, 1771.

think *"themselves obliged ...... to answer either his or the publications of any other individual"*, but nevertheless in the same issue issued a statement signed by Brindley and Simcox that the canal was laid out only in accord with the nature of the ground *"without any intention to benefit the Company at the expense of the Public"*.

Garbett answered Brindley's and Simcox's statement the following week by addressing several leading questions to Brindley. He asked, *"Was not the canal marked out in improper places where Brindley would not have taken it? Was not the canal longer than it ought to be? And did he not make some reservations when he put his name to the statement published in last week's Gazette"*. Garbett further added that Brindley had *"been heard frequently to express his great concern at the improper things which were done at the Birmingham Canal"*. A letter from Bentley was also published in the same issue and, after attacking Garbett's letters, claimed that the contract offered to Fownes was similar to those accepted by other coal masters, and that Nicklin had deceived the Company by offering to pay the extra expense of the canal going to their land then had refused when the work was under way.

By this time, the Gazette, having received *"a variety of complaints that my paper is filled with disputes relative to the Birmingham Navigation"*, decided it was time to end the controversy, although one final letter from Garbett concerning the Nicklin dispute was printed the following week. Although the dispute was removed from the pages of the Gazette, it was carried on fiercely within the town. In February a Committee of Trustees, including Garbett and Turner, was appointed at a meeting of the town to promote action against the Company, and to this end they presented a paper to the Company requesting that it give up part or all of the Brick-kiln Piece, on the payment of appropriate compensation, to the Trustees for the use of the town or parish. Representatives of the Trustees met the Canal Committee on 29th March to put forward their case during which Garbett informed the Committee that he intended to present a petition to Parliament over the Company's conduct.[103] The Company were unsure if Garbett meant what he said[104] but at a General Assembly on 5th April decided not to give up any of the Brick-kiln Piece to the Trustees and not even let go

---

103 The Gazette, 1st March, 1771.
104 The Gazette, 29th March, 1771.

the weighing machine or temporary wharf.[105] The Company's declared resolve seems to have worked for the available evidence from that moment on indicates that the opposition faded away and no evidence was found that Garbett did indeed petition Parliament.

Although entries in the Minute Books substantiate the Company's defence over Nicklin and Fownes, other entries indicate that they did indeed seek to establish a monopoly of the coal trade and were violating the terms of the Act. As in the Brick-kiln/Newhall Affair the Company throughout adopted a high-handed attitude and certainly an air of "Who will call us to account?" as suggested by Garbett's anonymous letter in the Gazette on 31st December 1770. As we shall see, the charges that the canal was lengthened extensively from that planned were absolutely true, but the reasons for the extensions are somewhat obscure. Never-the-less the dispute with the Nicklins demonstrates that the Company were prepared to extend the canal if they could gain or save money by such action; Garbett, who as an earlier member of the Committee, probably knew as well as anyone why extensions were made and he was convinced they were made for gain by the Company. The general attitude of the Company indicates that the opposition's allegations about reasons for the extensions were probably well founded. The Company, however, although they could continue to favour their own boats using the canal to try to establish a monopoly of the wharfs and coal trade, were never able to do so. The success of Colmore in Parliament meant that others who wished to erect wharfs and warehouses on their lands bordering the canal could do so, and the promotion of several private carrying companies, although working under many restrictions imposed by the Company, prevented a monopoly in the coal carrying trade. In this dispute the Company had won the battle but had failed to win the war to secure its monopolistic aims.

---

105 The Gazette, 5th April, 1771.

CHAPTER 9

JOURNEY'S END

WITH COALS arriving at the town and with the canal still uncompleted, the everyday running and building of the canal continued throughout the two disputes. The first task was to ensure that, now the canal was open to the collieries, there were sufficient boats and boatmen available to transport the coal to the town. A Mr. Beck was sent immediately "*to Brosely and Madely to endeavour to procure two proper persons to steer and three to stow the Company boats*",[106] and Garbett was "*requested to write to Mr. Gilbert at the Duke of Bridgewater's to lend the Company a boy or two to steer the boats*"[107] and also some boat builders.[108]

It was ordered that the number of Company boats be increased to 50 on 15th November and two days later "*that three more sheds for the building of boats be immediately erected*".[109] As contained in the Act the boats were 70 feet long, 7 feet wide and 3 feet 6 inches deep. Originally canal boats were built fitted with a mainsail but it was soon found that a sail was of little help and a single horse could draw a boat laden with 20 to 30 tons without any assistance. Horses were ordered to be used along the whole length of the canal on the Company's boats except through the locks, and there the boats were to be drawn in by the men.[110] From a recommendation by Brindley, the boats carried a lead strip marked and

---

106 C.M.B., 10th November, 1769.
107 C.M.B., 15th November, 1769.
108 C.M.B., 17th November, 1691.
109 C.M.B., 15th November, 1769.
110 C.M.B., 15th November, 1769.

divided into inches so that the water drawn, and consequently the weight of a boat's load, was known. Similar strips were put in the locks to show the depth of water in the lock, and by comparing the two sets of strips, in times of drought, damage to the lock could be avoided by refusing to allow a boat passage through unless there would be a clearance of one inch of water.[111] It was also found that standing in the bottom of the boat the steersmen found difficulty in seeing, and so stages were erected for them to stand on.[112]

With boats now *"constantly employed"*[113] provision had to be made for full time lock keepers to be employed at Smethwick. Four were employed altogether, working alternately day and night in pairs so that *"no delay or irregularity may be occasioned in the passage of the boats"*,[114] which suggests that the boats travelled through the night as well as through the day. The keepers were provided with houses consisting of *"a lower room, a chamber, and a pantry"*,[115] but had two shillings and sixpence (10½p) deducted from their wages as rent.

As we have seen in Chapter 6, with the opening of the canal the price of coal in the town fell to six shillings and eight pence per ton (33p) or four pence per cwt (1.6p). This, however, was the price at the temporary wharf, and the prices at other distribution points in and near the town were slightly higher, for example:

> *"at the coat yard the top of Friday Street, at 5d per cwt. Or 8/4 per ton; or by Mr. Baliss at Camp Hill, at 6d per hundred or 10/- per ton, clear of any expense of weighing etc."* [116]

On 5th March 1770 it was announced:

> *"As the inhabitants of this town have complained of the inconvenience of going to the wharf to order coals, the following places are appointed to received orders, which will be called for every evening and supplied with the utmost despatch."* [117]

---

111 C.M.B., 15th November, 1769.
112 C.M.B., 10th November, 1769.
113 C.M.B., 17th November, 1769.
114 C.M.B., 15th November, 1769.
115 C.M.B., 15th November, 1769.
116 C.M.B., 5th February, 1770.
117 C.M.B., 5th March, 1770.

Seven places were listed, including the navigation office in Newhall Street. It also added that the country teams from outside the town could be supplied at the wharf for seven shillings and six pence (37½p) per ton. That the country teams took full advantage of the offer can be seen, along with some other interesting points, in the following extract of a letter of 3rd February from John Ash to Lord Dartmouth:

> *"the canal is full of Boats belonging to the Company and private owners.....*
> *and coals are daily hawked about the streets for purchasers, the Town is fully*
> *stocked and the country teams increase on the Wharf, so that the wagons are*
> *very few indeed..... Three hundred Tons at least are brought daily by the*
> *Navigation, which is 100 Tons at least are brought daily by the Navigation,*
> *which is 100 tons more than the Town has demand for."* [118]

The Company accounts for this period show an increase from around 1,500 tons per week in April 1770 to well over 2,000 tons per week by the end of the year. There appeared to be 10 private carriers on the canal,[119] of which the largest was the Birmingham Boat Company. This company also sold coal in the town at 4d per cwt. and coke at one shilling three pence (6.1p) per sack, assuring the teams of a constant supply.[120] In a letter to James Watt that year a Dr Small stated that above *"150 boats are now employed"*.

The Company were always quick to take an opportunity to increase their profits and consequently they were prepared to carry or sell anything which would prove remunerative. An example of this can be seen in an advertisement in the Gazette on 12th March that the Company was aware that some persons were carrying away sand from the side of the canal at the Smethwick summit and, unless the same was paid for, prosecutions would follow.[121] Subsequently on 11th May the Company resolved to bring some of the sand to Birmingham to see if it could be sold at one shilling (5p) per cwt.[122]

With trade beginning, and perhaps in anticipation that their primary wharf was not to be at Newhall, the Company decided in March 1770[123] that the

---

118 Quoted by Hadfield, Canals of the West Midlands.
119 B.C.N. Journal.
120 The Gazette, 14th May, 1770.
121 The Gazette, 12th March, 1770.
122 C.M.B., 11th May, 1770.
123 B.C.N. Journal.

present office in Newhall Street was not big enough and so it was decided to plan and construct new offices which would include a General Assembly room, a Committee room, offices and houses for clerks *"and adjoining coffee house and Tavern for the accommodation of the meetings"*, the money to build it being raised by voluntary subscriptions.[124]

The Navigation Office 1783

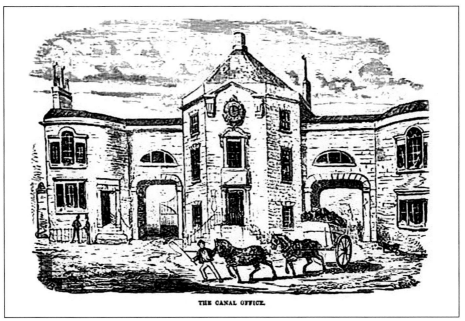

THE CANAL OFFICE.

The Navigation office was situated in Suffolk Street near the terminus of the canal wharf. It was enlarged and extended many time until its demolition in the 1920s.

The progress of the coal trade led to an expectation of high profits from the canal, and when shares were put on the market in January 1770 their value rose quickly. They had risen from £100 to £130 by February and by the end of that year reached £153, by the end of 1771 they were at £182, and by the end of 1772 they had reached £210. This rapid rise in the value of shares continued well into the next 20 years and by the July of 1792 they had reached £1170.[125] One shareholder in 1768, although he already had the maximum of ten shares, purchased a further ten. He was found out and the shares were confiscated, and

---

124 C.M.B., 30th March, 1770.
125 B.C.N. Journal.

sold by auction, the proceeds going into the Company.[126] Many shares were sold "by inch of candle", a method of auction whereby the last bid before a pin, which had been pushed into a candle one inch down from where the candle was lit, fell out was accepted as the winning bid.[127]

During the summer of 1770 a scheme for a rival canal to bring coals to Birmingham was formulated. The scheme was to bring a canal from Lichfield, through the coal areas around Walsall, untouched by the Birmingham canal, to Birmingham.[128] As Samuel Garbett was a leading figure in this scheme,[129] it may be that it was a by-product of his dispute with the Birmingham Canal Company and the fears of a coal monopoly by that Company. A meeting was held at Lichfield on 18th August where a committee, including Garbett, was elected and a subscription opened to carry out a survey.[130] The plan, however, met with much opposition from the local landowners and mill owners who would be affected by the scheme[131] and many of the subscribers wished to withdraw their subscriptions and the project was wound up by March 1771.[132] The original estimate for the cost to construct the canal had been £55,000 and another £15,000 in reserve to cover any possible increase. The actual cost, however, was £112,000 (equivalent to over £20 million in 2021) more than double the original estimate. Much of the increase must have been due to the increased length of the canal, but even taking this into account it is clear to see that the original estimate was over-optimistic. The first £15,000 of the extra cost was raised, as allowed by the Act, through a shares issue, which gave each share a value of £140, the balance being raised by loans. The plan however was revived in outline much later as the Birmingham and Fazeley canal.

Plan of the Canals between Liverpool, Bristol and Hull

News of other canals often appeared in the columns of the Gazette and the edition of 16th July, 1770, gave an account of the progress at that time in canal construction:

---

126 The Gazette, 19th March, 1768.
127 The Gazette, 19th March, 1770.
128 The Gazette, 6th August, 1770.
129 The Gazette, 29th October, 1770.
130 The Gazette, 27th August, 1770.
131 The Gazette, 19th March, 1768.
132 The Gazette, 18th March, 1771.

Account of the canals now finished cutting, and intended to be cut, from Liverpool to different parts of the Kingdom.

THE GRAND TRUNK	MILES
From the Mersey near Runcorn to near Oxford, which will be completed in four Years	182
Finished a branch to the Severn, near Bewdley	44
Finished a branch to the Trent, near Wilden Ferry	33
A branch to Coventry	6
Finished a branch to Birmingham	24
Finished a branch to Droitwich	5
Will be finished in two years a Branch Duke of Bridgewater's To Manchester	40
Finished Sankey canal	16
Will be finished in eight years, Leeds Canal	120
	470
Intended a branch from Leeds to Kendall and Lancaster	60
Intended a branch to Manchester, by Chorley and Wigan, from Near Preston	40
	570

There are some inaccuracies in the information given, the most obvious here being that the Birmingham canal was not yet finished. The Droitwich canal was not finished until March 1771[133] and the Staffordshire and Worcestershire canal was not finished to near Bewdley until March 1771.[134] At that time Bewdley was an important and thriving township on the River Severn. The townsfolk however, and presumably some of the River Severn boat people, were opposed to a canal terminating in the town and so the canal was taken to the Severn at a point below Bewdley where the small river Stour joined it. The success of the canal eventually resulted in a new town growing up around the junction, Stourport, and which soon became a more thriving and important town while Bewdley's prosperity and importance declined.

---

133 The Gazette, 18th March, 1771.
134 The Gazette, 1st April, 1771.

Construction of the Birmingham canal continued apace with the main aim being to secure enough water to maintain the whole length of the canal when completed. Work on the two reservoirs started in 1769, and on 11th November of that year Brindley advised that the dam at Smethwick should be immediately strengthened and raised, as it was not by then sufficiently secure.[135] After Simcox had consulted the mill owners above the reservoir it was raised between 4 and 6 feet, and Boulton and Small reported in February 1770 that *"the supply will be very considerable and that one other such will effectively secure the canal against any want of water"*.[136] One of the problems at the reservoirs was leakage and to solve the problem Brindley recommended that *"cattle be put to graze about the edges of the pool to tread in the soil, and muddy the water, which would seal the leak as it settled"*.[137]

Despite frequent damage to the works, for example, in October 1769 and August 1770 (perhaps due to sheer vandalism or perhaps a reflection of the opposition to the Company still prominent in the town at this time), the canal proceeded steadily towards Autherley. Preparations for the Junction had begun very early. In November 1769, Brindley, apprehending that water would be in short supply beyond Bilston, had determined that to save water the locks that fell down to Autherley would all be three feet locks (ie. with a fall and lift of three feet) except the extreme lock which would be six feet.[138] Bricks for the locks were sought in January 1770[139] and wood in May 1770[140], Brindley advising that 600,000 bricks should be provided that summer for the Autherley locks.[141]

By May the canal was completed to Tipton, apart from the towing paths,[142] and by August Bilston had obviously been reached as Simcox was ordered to set out the line from *"Bilston to the first lock at Autherley"*.[143] Although they were given assurances by Brindley of the work being done,[144] the Staffordshire and Worcestershire Canal Company were not satisfied with the progress being

---

135 C.M.B., 11th November, 1769.
136 C.M.B., 2nd February, 1770.
137 C.M.B., 24th May, 1771.
138 C.M.B., 11th November, 1769.
139 C.M.B., 26th January, 1770.
140 C.M.B., 11th May, 1770.
141 C.M.B., 25th April, 1770.
142 C.M.B., 18th May, 1770.
143 C.M.B., 13th August, 1770.
144 C.M.B., 16th August, 1770.

made. That Company advertised in December that there was to be a general meeting to decide whether to petition Parliament to order the completion of the Junction as laid down in the terms of the Birmingham Act (which said the Junction should be made within 6 months of the canal reaching Birmingham from the coal pits).[145] The Birmingham Company complained that they were doing everything in their power to effect the Junction[146] but the Staffordshire and Worcestershire Company were not satisfied and applied for a bill to make the junction themselves. This was a particularly bad time for the Birmingham Company as the dispute over their monopoly attempts was at its peak and Colmore had a bill going before Parliament over the Newhall termination. Not wanting to add to their difficulties the Company quickly submitted to the Staffordshire and Worcestershire Company, paying all the costs of their legal procedure and promising to hurry the completion of the Junction. The Earl of Dartmouth also gave his assistance pacifying the other Company.[147]

In order to keep the promise of a rapid completion of the Junction, in April 1771 three million more bricks were ordered for the locks, and all available planks and barrows to be sent to Autherley.[148] By 19th August the canal was opened as far as Wolverhampton.[149] Although some delay was occasioned by the necessity of completing the canal at Birmingham to Newhall, Brindley was able to report on 27th March 1772 that it was completed before the date set out in Colmore's act.[150] The rush to Autherley was probably the cause of the locks there being, according to Brindley, *"very badly executed"* but they were quickly righted[151] for in 1772 on 14th September the waters of the Birmingham canal finally mingled with those of the Staffordshire and Worcestershire canal. The meeting of the waters of the two canals marked the completion of the first Birmingham canal.

The completed canal was 22⅝ miles in length. Brindley's original plan intended a canal only 16½ miles long, an increase of nearly one third from that planned. The distance from Birmingham to Autherley, as the crow flies,

---

145 The Gazette, 3rd December, 1770.
146 The Gazette, 10th December, 1770.
147 C.M.B., 1st March, 1771.
148 C.M.B., 16th April, 1771.
149 The Gazette, 19th August, 1771.
150 C.M.B., 27th March, 1772.
151 C.M.B., 18th May, 1772.

is little more than 12 miles. The increase in length over Brindley's original plan seems to suggest that the circuitous route of the canal to Autherley was not entirely due to Brindley's method of following the contours of the land. It also provides much validity to the allegations that the length of the canal was increased, or was allowed to be increased, because the Company levied tolls by the mile travelled.

The completion of the canal to Autherley did not bring any sharp increase in the tonnage carried on the canal, in fact entries in the Company's ledgers show a fall after the junction was made:

5th September   Carried 2641 tons 6 cwt.   Tolls £155. 9s. 10d.
3rd October   Carried 2033 tons 18 cwt.   Tolls £137.16s. 0d.

(NB: The slight drop in revenue compared to the large drop in tonnage shows that the tonnage was being carried a greater distance, a clear indication that the junction was being used).

The fall, however, was only temporary, and tonnage from then on rose steadily. The reasons why there was not a sharp increase in tonnage with the junction being opened were: (1) The line to Liverpool was not completed until 1777; (2) and stemming from (1) only tonnage for Bristol could pass along the canal and, as was shown in Chapters 3 and 4, this would mean mainly light manufactured goods, hence no substantial increase in tonnage could be expected. The main tonnage carried on the canal continued to be coal and it was probably a fluctuation in this commodity that caused the drop after the junction was opened. All of this also indicates why the Company was not particularly concerned about making the junction to Autherley as soon as possible, for the real benefits of the junction were not to be realised for several years.

The completed canal constituted two firsts: it was the first canal to Birmingham; and it was the first canal which linked as a branch to another without a junction to a navigable river at some point along it. Unfortunately the canal was also a 'last' as on 5th October 1772, the Gazette announced:

"On Sunday the 27th September last died at his house at Turnhurst in Staffordshire, that eminent mechanic and engineer, Mr James Brindley, of whom it may be truly said: he has not lived in vain."

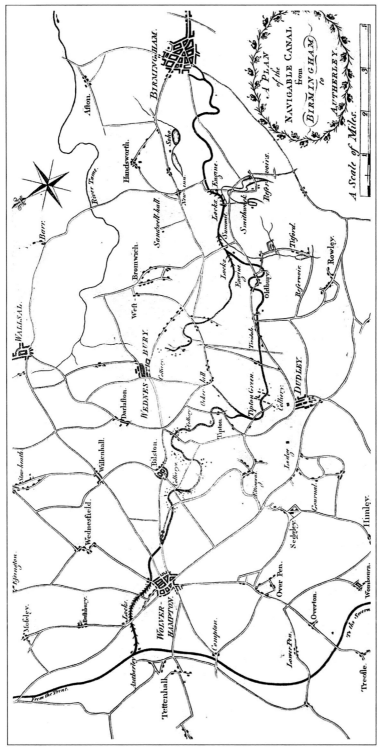

Plan of the Canals between Liverpool, Bristol and Hull, Circa 1770.

Only two days earlier the Company had notified Brindley that he would be released from their service on 29th September, and so on the date of his death he was still officially in the employment of the Company whose canal he had completed only two weeks earlier.[152]

The canal was to play a vital part in the later progress and enormous development of Birmingham into the City it is now. The canal had come at a time when Birmingham's industries, trade and growth were in danger of stagnation, if not decline, because of a lack of cheap transport facilities which from that time have always been of prime importance to the town. By providing the first basis for cheap transport facilities to and from the town and so ensuring the town's future growth in all respects Birmingham's debt to its first canal and its engineer truly cannot be overestimated.

'It was a pleasing and flattering sight to an Englishman, at this remotest part of the globe, to see that Wedgwood's stoneware, and Birmingham goods, had found their way into the shops of Coupang.'

George Hamilton, Surgeon of HMS Pandora,
1791, Coupang, East Timor, Indonesia.

---

152 C.M.B., 22nd September, 1772.

APPENDICES

APPENDIX 1

Names of proprietors named in the original Act of Parliament

Earl of Hertford
Earl of Dartmouth
Sir Lister Holt
Charles Colmore
Ann Colmore
Thomas Anson
John Sneyd
Jervoise Clarke
Henry Carver
Peter Capper
Matthew Boulton
John Turner/Junior
John Kettle
Samuel Garbett
Charles Gascoigne
Samuel Galton
Joseph Wilkinson
William Welch
John Lane
Daniel Ruston
Joseph Ruston
John Hale
Maria Lhuile
Thomas Westley
Daniel Winwood
Rachel Swadlin
Sarah Johnson

John Meredith
/Junior
Joseph Geast
Thomas Bagnall
Thomas Silvester
/Junior
John Whitehouse
Richard Wright
Henry Venner
Samuel Pemberton
Joseph Oakley
Phebe Meredith
Sarah Whitehouse
William Hunt
John Grew
Thomas Russell
William Turner
Henry Carver
/Junior
John Wright
John Wall
John Ash M.D.
William Jones
John Baker
James Perry
James Cooper
Edward Carver

Richard Jesson
Mary Jesson
Benjamin Brett
John Oseland
Thomas Highway
John Lee
Richard Parkes
John Francis
Michael Lakin
Hannah Perkins
John Gibbons
James Dallaway
John Cope
Joseph Baarker
William Butler
Thomas Salt
Peter Capper/Junior
Mary Rider
John Kirkman
Thomas Wardid
Rebecca Jerson
Willis Kempson
John Hanson
James Farquharson
Thomas Lee
John Scott
John Moody

Richard Rabone
John Gold
William Grice
John Startin
Elias Wallins
Joseph Cotterill
William
Small, M.D.
William
John Banner
Francis
Farquharson
John Iddins/Junior
John Meredith
/Junior
Thomas Allen
Edward Palmer
Elisabeth Savage
Mary Savage
Ann Savage
John Turton
John Alston
Isaac Whitehouse
Richard Aston
Thomas Hanson
Henry Venour
John Bickley

APPENDIX 2

A letter from Dr Small to James Watt on 17th July 1770 says that he and Boulton *"are very desirous of so to move canal boats by this engine"*, (referring of course to Watt's steam engine) and that they have prepared a model of a boat for him. He continues that, as *"coals here are exceedingly cheap"*, a condenser will not be necessary, and that the field for such boats is not narrow, for *"above 150 boats are now employed"*. *"Fire engines"* (steam engines) he adds, may also be used to supply the locks with water, and *"if your reciprocator can be ready, let is be so."*

The letter contains some interesting information. It shows Boulton's developing interest at this time in Watt and his engine, and his awareness of its potential to provide motive power. This in itself is of great interest, for it not only suggests the use of a steam engine that can transmit a rotary motion; it must also be one of the very early positive notions for providing a purely mechanical drive for boats.

It shows that, to Small at least, the full implications of the condenser were not fully appreciated and that it was regarded primarily as a means of saving fuel. Taking away the condenser and leaving the engine basically the same would not have affected its fuel consumption at all, and so it seems that Small was advocating a return to an atmospheric type engine.

* * *

Another item of interest in the connection of Watt and the Canal Company is that among the shareholders in 1771 appears the name of James Pickard, the Birmingham man alleged to have stolen the idea of the crank from Watt for converting the reciprocating movement of the steam engine to rotary movement.

APPENDIX 3

For many years the Author travelled the English and Welsh canals in a narrowboat, the 'Phoenix'. Here he tells the story behind that narrowboat.

The Rise of the Phoenix

In the early 1960s a wooden butty boat came to the end of its working life of carrying ash waste from midland Power Stations to various dumps. As so often happened back then the old butty was cut into two parts to be sold off as two shorter boats. An early pioneering chap from Rugeley, whose name I sadly can't remember, bought one of these parts to restore it as a boat for cruising.

After designing, making and bolting on a full width paddle gear to the rear sawn off end, he built a full length cabin and took to cruising the waterways under the name of the 'Water Rambler'. His power source was an engine extracted from an Austin 7 complete with gearbox and back axle which then connected to a Mississippi style paddle at the rear. In the early days of so-called 'pleasure cruising' it was a prime example of the creative powers of the under funded which would put Heath Robinson himself into the shade and shallow waters of a winding hole.

When this pioneer bought the shortened hull he was told that the boat had been built in 1898 and the weary condition of the hulk made this more than slightly feasible. Whatever its true age, however, its tired old planks could not take the thrashing meted out by the heavy weight paddle fabricated from angle iron and builders' planks. Perhaps inevitably, the newly mobile hulk soon began to take in water at an unacceptably high rate. Something had to be done and so our optimistic pioneer decided that he would seal the newly sprung leaks from the inside of the hull using a mixture of dogged determination and boiling tar. Perhaps to soothe his many anxieties he did this while smoking a lighted cigarette! The inevitable happened, and by the time the local fire brigade had doused the raging flames his cherished cabin was no more and the hull was left somewhat charred and forlorn. Our now demoralised and despondent pioneer reluctantly decided enough was enough and decided to sell the Rambler very cheaply to a passing idiot, namely yours truly, at that time another totally under funded canal nutter.

My father, Tommy Dawson, came from an old canal family and he himself had been born on a boat somewhere on the Grand Union Canal. He had spent the whole of his working life on the 'cut' finally ending up manhandling the scoop on a horse pulled dredger and owned by Padget and Son who were based on the Tame Valley Canal at the bottom of the Perry Barr flight. Rather sensibly, although perhaps a little too late, I sought his venerable advice on how to seal and repair leaks on a wooden hull. He informed me that the time honoured method was to ram, preferably from the outside, a mixture of tar and horse manure into any leaks or cracks liable to leak. So indeed that is exactly what I did.

After carefully mixing well-dried horse manure with boiling tar heated by an old paraffin primus stove, I stuffed this medieval equivalent of fibre glass into any hole or rotting wood I found. For those of you who are anxious or mad enough to want to try this yourselves, you must use very, very dry horse manure otherwise it froths and grows like an impending volcanic eruption. I digress. The charred hull was scraped and wire brushed to eventually produce a rather pleasing effect. It was time to start building the cabin.

The cabin was built using ex-railway workshop floor boards for the main supports and household floor boarding rescued from Birmingham's slum clearance programme for the roof and sides. The roof was double planked and sealed by another of my dad's time honoured methods of spreading gallons of old paint across layers of cloth and newspapers to be finally topped off with canvas sheeting. That roof never leaked!

It was time now to consider mobility. The ingenious paddle gear, engine and gearbox were replaced by a 75hp Evinrude outboard engine and the restored hulk was able to go cruising again managing, with care, nearly five miles to an imperial gallon.

More advice from my dad. He told me that an old boatman's belief was that if you change a boat's name you change its luck. As under the name of 'Water Rambler' the boat had experienced some seriously bad luck, it seemed to be at least worth a try, but what to call her? At that time the boat, along with one other, was moored above Curdworth top Lock on the Birmingham and Fazeley Canal. The other boat was a converted ex-army pontoon belonging to Don Clive and his family (Don later became the Lock Keeper at Curdworth). On hearing of my plight and with little hesitation Don announced that there could only be one name for a boat that had risen not once but twice from the ashes and that name was Phoenix. And so it was.

Propelled by the high-revving very ungreen Evinrude the Phoenix's early voyages included attending boat rallies, indeed it's first journey, with my dad on board, was to the re-opening of the Dudley Tunnel in 1973 and then the following year to the Teme Valley. The healing properties of tar and horse muck however are somewhat limited and after pumping out a sunken Phoenix several times at her mooring it was too obvious that the old wooden hull had a terminal condition from which there was no hope of recovery. Incidentally, each time she sank my dad would reassure me that 'it will do her good' as the water would swell the planks and thus eliminate the leaks. This was true but in the process I would be left with water-clogged and ruined furnishings. I decided that drastic surgery was called for to ensure that the Phoenix would rise from the waters no more. I devised a plan to keep my newly built and well loved cabin and to replace the deteriorating wooden hull with a brand new steel one!

The relatively new Springer Engineering Company took on the task to build me a steel hull to my specifications at what old Sam Springer himself assured me was 'a ******* good price' and it included delivery to the British Waterways Yard at Fazeley. It arrived very soon afterwards and, after a launching ceremony involving a bottle of Babycham, was dropped into the water. From there it was hauled and poled (the towpath was impassable in places back then) up to the top of Curdworth locks to be readied for its next reincarnation. The cabin was freed from its fixings to the wooden hull and jacked up a few inches above it and then guided into a full Curdworth top lock. Once in the lock steel bars were pushed through the cabin-hull gap so that they protruded on either side of the lock. When all was in place under the watchful eye of Joe Siddles, the then lock keeper, the lock was very carefully and slowly emptied. Once empty the wooden hull was hauled out and the new steel hull hauled in below the hanging cabin. The gates were closed, the paddles lifted and the new hull rose rather majestically to pick up the hanging cabin on its way! The cabin was jacked up again, the steel bars removed and the cabin lowered into place. It fitted perfectly; Sam Springer had done his job well. The whole process in the lock took less than an hour, and it really was as simple as it sounds.

I had had the new hull built to a length of fifty feet which was twelve feet longer than the wooden hull it was replacing. This enabled me to add another length of cabin made to resemble an original boatman's cabin. A 1.5 BMC diesel, rescued from a breaker's yard for the princely sum of ten pounds replaced the Evinrude, and was linked to the propeller via a prop shaft. The engine was cooled via a car radiator which at times of hot weather required a regular drenching of cold water to help out. Later in the early eighties funds allowed for the professional installation of a PRM gear box and cooling tanks by Rose Narrowboats and so at long last the restoration of the Phoenix was complete.

The Phoenix served me well. For over twenty years my wife Tricia and I travelled most of England's navigable canals and rivers. At various times the Phoenix was homebased at Curdworth Top lock, Norbury Junction, Thrupp, Stourport Basin, and Great Bedwyn. When repainting her I always kept one side as showing her re-birth home of Curdworth while the other would show her current home base. With retirement and impending old age I rather reluctantly sold her in 1995 and that part of my life came to an end although the memories live on.

The Phoenix at Newbury.

BIBLIOGRAPHY

GENERAL WORKS

The First Industrial Revolution, Phyllis Deane, 1965
Economic History of Modern Britain, J. Clapham, 1926
River Navigation in England 1600-1750, T.S. Willan, 1964
Lives of the Engineers, S. Smiles, 1861
Matthew Boulton, H.W. Dickenson, 1937
Studies in The Industrial Revolution, edited by L. Pressnell, 1960
English Historical Documents, Volume 10

WORKS RELATING TO BIRMINGHAM

The History of Birmingham, 1783, W. Hutton, 1783
Old and New Birmingham, 1880, R. Dent, 1880
History of Birmingham, C. Gill, 1838
Birmingham and its Regional Setting, 1950, Brit. Assoc. Adv. Sci., 1950

WORKS RELATING TO CANALS

British Canals, C. Hadfield, 1950
Canals of the West Midlands, C. Hadfield, 1968
General History of Inland Navigation, J. Phillips, 1795
The B.C.N. in Pictures, B.C.N. Society, 1973
The Birmingham Canal Navigations, R.H. Davies, 2010
Birmingham's Canals, R. Schill, 1999

PRIMARY SOURCES

Birmingham Canal Navigation's Minute Books, Ledgers and Journals

Aris's Birmingham Gazette from 1760 until 1772

A View of the Advantages of Inland Navigation 1766 by Bentley

The Advantages of Inland Navigation 1766 by Whitworth

A Collection of Letters relating to Boulton and Watt collected by Timmins

Miscellaneous Documents relating to Matthew Boulton 1762-1807

Acts of Parliament

Wedgwood Correspondence

Sketchley and Adams Directory, 1767

Pye's Directory, 1767

Collection of letters of James Watt to Matthew Boulton and Dr Small, 1768 until 1774

Voyage of HMS Pandora, Captain E. Edwards, G. Hamilton, 1791

A great many single documents in the Birmingham Reference Library.